THE ANNOTATED SHAKESPEARE

A Midsummer Night's Dream

William Shakespeare

Fully annotated, with an Introduction, by Burton Raffel
With an essay by Harold Bloom

THE ANNOTATED SHAKESPEARE

Burton Raffel, General Editor

Yale University Press • *New Haven and London*

Designed by Rebecca Gibb.
Set in Bembo type by The Composing Room of Michigan, Inc.
Printed in the United States of America by R. R. Donnelley & Sons.

Library of Congress Cataloging-in-Publication Data
Shakespeare, William, 1564–1616.
A Midsummer Night's Dream / William Shakespeare ; fully annotated,
with an introduction, by Burton Raffel ; with an essay by Harold Bloom.
p.   cm.
Includes bibliographical references.
ISBN 0-300-10653-X (pbk.)
1. Theseus (Greek mythology)—Drama.   2. Hippolyta (Greek mythology)—Drama.   3. Athens (Greece)—Drama.   4. Courtship—
Drama.   I. Raffel, Burton.   II. Title.
PR2827.A2R34   2005
822.3'3—dc22
2004024958

A catalogue record for this book is available from the British Library.

10 9 8 7 6 5 4 3 2 1

For Yehuda Yair Pride

CONTENTS

ABOUT THIS BOOK

In act 5, scene 1, Hippolyta and her future husband, Theseus, conduct the following exchange:

Hippolyta 'Tis strange my Theseus, that these lovers speak of.
Theseus   More strange than true. I never may believe
  These antique fables, nor these fairy toys.
  Lovers and madmen have such seething brains,
  Such shaping fantasies, that apprehend
  More than cool reason ever comprehends.
  The lunatic, the lover and the poet
  Are of imagination all compact.
  One sees more devils than vast hell can hold:
  That is the madman. The lover, all as frantic,
  Sees Helen's beauty in a brow of Egypt.
  The poet's eye, in a fine frenzy, rolling,
  Doth glance from heaven to earth, from earth to heaven.
  And as imagination bodies forth
  The forms of things unknown, the poet's pen
  Turns them to shapes and gives to airy nothing
  A local habitation, and a name.

Such tricks hath strong imagination,

That if it would but apprehend some joy,

It comprehends some bringer of that joy.

Or in the night, imagining some fear,

How easy is a bush supposed a bear?

(lines 1–22)

This was perfectly understandable, we must assume, to the mostly very average persons who paid to watch Elizabethan plays. But who today can make much sense of it? In this very fully annotated edition, I therefore present this passage, not in the bare form quoted above, but thoroughly supported by bottom-of-the-page notes:

Hippolyta 'Tis strange my Theseus, that[1] these lovers speak of.

Theseus More strange than true. I never may[2] believe

These antique fables,[3] nor these fairy toys.[4]

Lovers and madmen have such seething[5] brains,

Such shaping[6] fantasies, that apprehend[7]

More than cool reason ever comprehends.

The lunatic, the lover and the poet

Are of imagination all compact.[8]

One sees more devils than vast hell can hold:

1 that which
2 can
3 antique fables = old / old-fashioned legendary / mythological fiction, falsehoods, nonsense
4 idle / fantastic tales
5 boiling, tumultuous, ceaselessly agitated
6 formative / creative
7 learn, perceive, understand, become conscious of
8 (1) composed, (2) linked closely together

That is the madman. The lover, all[9] as frantic,[10]
Sees Helen's beauty in a brow of Egypt.[11]
The poet's eye, in a fine frenzy,[12] rolling,
Doth glance from heaven to earth, from earth to heaven.
And as imagination bodies forth[13]
The forms of things unknown, the poet's pen
Turns them to shapes and gives to airy nothing
A local habitation,[14] and a name.
Such tricks[15] hath strong imagination,[16]
That[17] if it would but[18] apprehend some joy,
It comprehends[19] some bringer of that joy.
Or[20] in the night, imagining some fear,
How easy is a bush supposed a bear?

The modern reader or listener may well better understand this intensely sarcastic speech in context, as the play continues. But without full explanation of words that have over the years shifted in meaning, and usages that have been altered, neither the modern reader nor the modern listener is likely to be equipped for anything like the full comprehension that Shakespeare intended and all readers or listeners deserve.

9 every bit
10 wild, raging
11 brow of Egypt = dark/gypsy face
12 fine frenzy = pure/consummate/elevated delirium/mania
13 bodies forth = embodies, gives shape to
14 local habitation = spatial position, dwelling, residence
15 devices, stratagems
16 iMAgiNAsiON
17 so that
18 would but = only
19 grasps, understands
20 in the same way

I believe annotations of this sort create the necessary bridges from Shakespeare's four-centuries-old English across to ours. Some readers, to be sure, will be able to comprehend unusual, historically different meanings without glosses. Those not familiar with the modern meaning of particular words will easily find clear, simple definitions in any modern dictionary. But most readers are not likely to understand Shakespeare's intended meaning, absent such glosses as I here offer.

My annotation practices have followed the same principles used in *The Annotated Milton,* published in 1999, and in my annotated editions of *Hamlet,* published (as the initial volume in this series) in 2003, and *Romeo and Juliet* (published in 2004). Classroom experience has validated these editions. Classes of mixed upper-level undergraduates and graduate students have more quickly and thoroughly transcended language barriers than ever before. This allows the teacher, or a general reader without a teacher, to move more promptly and confidently to the non-linguistic matters that have made Shakespeare and Milton great and important poets.

It is the inevitable forces of linguistic change, operant in all living tongues, which have inevitably created such wide degrees of obstacles to ready comprehension—not only sharply different meanings, but subtle, partial shifts in meaning that allow us to think we understand when, alas, we do not. Speakers of related languages like Dutch and German also experience this shifting of the linguistic ground. Like early Modern English (ca. 1600) and the Modern English now current, those languages are too close for those who know only one language, and not the other, to be readily able always to recognize what they correctly understand

and what they do not. When, for example, a speaker of Dutch says, "Men kofer is kapot," a speaker of German will know that something belonging to the Dutchman is broken (*kapot* = "ka-putt" in German, and *men* = "mein"). But without more linguistic awareness than the average person is apt to have, the German speaker will not identify "kofer" ("trunk" in Dutch) with "Kör-per"—a modern German word meaning "physique, build, body." The closest word to "kofer" in modern German, indeed, is "Scrankkoffer," which is too large a leap for ready comprehension. Speakers of different Romance languages (such as French, Spanish, or Italian), and all other related but not identical tongues, all experience these difficulties, as well as the difficulty of understanding a text written in their own language five, or six, or seven hundred years earlier. Shakespeare's English is not yet so old that it requires, like many historical texts in French and German, or like Old English texts—for example, *Beowulf*—a modern translation. Much poetry evaporates in translation: language is immensely particular. The sheer sound of Dante in thirteenth-century Italian is profoundly worth preserving. So too is the sound of Shakespeare.

I have annotated prosody (metrics) only when it seemed truly necessary or particularly helpful. Except in the few instances where modern usage syllabifies the "e," whenever an "e" in Shakespeare is *not* silent, it is marked "è". The notation used for prosody, which is also used in the explanation of Elizabethan pronunciation, follows the extremely simple form of my *From Stress to Stress: An Autobiography of English Prosody* (see "Further Reading," near the end of this book). Syllables with metrical stress are capitalized; all other syllables are in lowercase letters. I have managed to employ normalized Elizabethan spellings, in most indications of pronunciation, but I have sometimes been obliged to deviate, in the higher interest of being understood.

I have annotated, as well, a limited number of such other matters, sometimes of interpretation, sometimes of general or historical relevance, as have seemed to me seriously worthy of inclusion. These annotations have been most carefully restricted: this is not intended to be a book of literary commentary. It is for that reason that the glossing of metaphors has been severely restricted. There is almost literally no end to discussion and/or analysis of metaphor, especially in Shakespeare. To yield to temptation might well be to double or triple the size of this book—and would also change it from a historically oriented language guide to a work of an unsteadily mixed nature. In the process, I believe, neither language nor literature would be well or clearly served.

Since the original printed texts of (there not being, as there never are for Shakespeare, any surviving manuscripts) are frequently careless as well as self-contradictory, I have been relatively free with the wording of stage directions—and in some cases have added brief directions, to indicate who is speaking to whom. I have made no emendations; I have necessarily been obliged to make choices. Textual decisions have been annotated when the differences between or among the original printed texts seem either marked or of unusual interest.

In the interests of compactness and brevity, I have employed in my annotations (as consistently as I am able) a number of stylistic and typographical devices:

- The annotation of a single word does not repeat that word

- The annotation of more than one word repeats the words

being annotated, which are followed by an equals sign and then by the annotation; the footnote number in the text is placed after the last of the words being annotated

- In annotations of a single word, alternate meanings are usually separated by commas; if there are distinctly different ranges of meaning, the annotations are separated by arabic numerals inside parentheses—(1), (2), and so on; in more complexly worded annotations, alternative meanings expressed by a single word are linked by a forward slash, or solidus: /

- Explanations of textual meaning are not in parentheses; comments about textual meaning are

- Except for proper nouns, the word at the beginning of all annotations is in lower case

- Uncertainties are followed by a question mark, set in parentheses: (?)

- When particularly relevant, "translations" into twenty-first-century English have been added, in parentheses

- Annotations of repeated words are not repeated. Explanations of the first instance of such common words are followed by the sign *. Readers may easily track down the first annotation, using the brief Finding List at the back of the book. Words with entirely separate meanings are annotated only for meanings no longer current in Modern English.

The most important typographical device here employed is the sign * placed after the first (and only) annotation of words and phrases occurring more than once. There is an alphabetically arranged listing of such words and phrases in the Finding List at the back of the book. The Finding List contains no annotations but simply gives the words or phrases themselves and the numbers of the relevant act, the scene within that act, and the footnote number within that scene for the word's first occurrence.

This Text

For most of Shakespeare's plays, there are competing contemporary printed versions. (There are no manuscript versions of any of the plays.) Editorial judgment, in such situations, is frequently not an option, but a necessity.

But *Dream* has only one authoritative contemporary text, the 1600 Quarto. Inevitably, there are typographical (and perhaps other errors) in the Quarto; these are for the most part noted, here, and sometimes discussed in the annotations to particular words and passages. Some lesser errors are corrected in the 1623 Folio and a very few in the 1619 Second Quarto. The twenty-first-century editor must be cautious about tampering with an essentially unique textual source, four hundred years old.

Spelling is not on the whole a basic issue, but punctuation and lineation must be given high respect. The First Quarto uses few exclamation marks or semicolons, which is to be sure a matter of the conventions of a very different era. Still, our modern preferences cannot be lightly substituted for what is, after a fashion, the closest thing to a Shakespeare manuscript we are likely ever to have. We do not know whether these particular seventeenth-century printers, like most of that time, were responsible for question marks, commas, periods and, especially, all-purpose colons, or whether these particular printers tried to follow their handwritten sources. Nor do we know if those sources, or what part thereof, might have been in Shakespeare's own hand, or even whether those sources were accurate representations of what

Shakespeare wrote, either in the first version of the play, in 1595, or in the later, revised versions that appear to have been produced. But in spite of these equivocations and uncertainties, it remains true that, to a very considerable extent, punctuation tends to result from just how the mind responsible for that punctuating *hears* the text. And twenty-first century minds have no business, in such matters, overruling seventeenth-century ones. Whoever the compositors were, they were more or less Shakespeare's contemporaries, and we are not.

Accordingly, when the First Quarto text uses a comma, we are being signaled that *they* (whoever "they" were) did not hear the text coming to a syntactic stop but continuing to some later stopping point. To replace Quarto commas with editorial periods is thus risky and, in a lyrically textured play, on the whole an undesirable practice. (The dramatic action of a tragedy may require us, for twenty-first-century readers, to highlight what four-hundred-year-old punctuation standards may not make clear—and may even, at times, misrepresent. But *Dream* is a complex comedy, in the formal Elizabethan sense of comedic, and its appreciation therefore depends less on action than on a blending of narrative and meditation. Verbal rhythms thus have a prominence, in *Dream,* that they do not have, say, in *Romeo and Juliet,* for all that *Romeo* is justly considered to be richly poetic. So too, for that matter, is *Hamlet* richly poetic—but its presentation of dramatic action is, like *Romeo*'s, bound into a quite different verbal texture.)

When the First Quarto text has a colon, what we are being signaled is that *they* heard a syntactic stop—though not necessarily or even usually the particular kind of syntactic stop we associate, today, with the colon. It is therefore inappropriate, in a lyrical drama like *Dream,* to substitute editorial commas for Quarto colons. It is also inappropriate to employ editorial colons when *their* syntactic usage of colons does not match ours. In general, the closest thing to *their* syntactic sense of the colon is our (and their) period.

The Quarto's interrogation (question) marks, too, merit extremely respectful handling in a play like *Dream*. In particular, editorial exclamation marks should very rarely be substituted for the Quarto's interrogation marks. The exclamation marks of the Quarto should of course be preserved.

It follows from these considerations that the movement and sometimes the meaning of what we must take to be Shakespeare's *Dream* will at times be different, depending on whose punctuation we follow, *theirs* or our own. I have tried to use the First Quarto's seventeenth-century text as a guide to both *hearing* and *understanding* what Shakespeare wrote.

There has never been much question that *A Midsummer Night's Dream* is delightful. Probably written and first performed in 1595, though we have no clear proof of either dating, it is usually viewed from two main perspectives: first, as an examination of the nature and intensity of the rare and often exalted delight it gives us, and second, as a kind of turning point in the overall development of Shakespeare as a dramatist. These are accurate and useful approaches. Yet I do not think an analysis of *Dream*'s many delights, in particular, takes us anything like as far as we need to go, for a full appreciation of the play. Both its pleasures and its achievement are based in profound and broad-ranging complexities—of characterization, of narrative and structure, of language—which are the furthest thing from light or happily inconsequential. The play's intensity is primarily lyrical, which necessarily changes both its overall texture and the relative prominence given to poetic meditation as contrasted with dramatic action. But no one would suggest, I think, that the lyrics of Shakespeare's younger contemporary, John Donne, are light and happily inconsequential. When Harold C. Goddard, one of the most dependably sensible of Shakespearean critics, calls *Dream*

"one of the lightest and in many respects the most purely playful of Shakespeare's plays," he perpetuates a long-standing tradition of miscomprehension (*Meaning of Shakespeare,* 1:74). I want to demonstrate in some detail why such simplistic approaches do not do justice to a resplendent lyrical drama that, like all great lyricism, is chock-full of social and psychological wisdom of the most serious sort.

Characterization

The numerical total of a play's cast of characters is usually irrelevant, especially in Elizabethan drama. *Dream* and the two plays that immediately precede it, *Romeo and Juliet* and *Richard II,* are generally agreed to be the first of Shakespeare's incontestably great dramas. These three plays have, respectively, Dramatis Personae of twenty-two, twenty-six, and twenty-three named roles. But among the three plays, the gradations of importance, from lead to supporting and, finally, to minor (that is, more than merely walk-on but less significant and much less developed) roles, are exceedingly unlike. *Romeo and Juliet* has just two lead roles (Romeo and Juliet), though Juliet's Nurse, Friar Lawrence, and Mercutio have large supporting parts, and there are three other supporting roles (Paris, Benvolio, and Tybalt). *Richard II* has two lead roles (Richard and Bolingbroke), plus three supporting roles (York, Isabel, and the Duchess of Gloucester). But *Dream* has nine lead roles (Theseus, Lysander, Demetrius, Bottom, Hermia, Helena, Oberon, Titania, and Puck)—or, if we choose to say that there are in fact no lead roles whatever, the play then has twelve supporting roles (adding Egeus, Quince, and Hippolyta). The precise gradations are not important. However, the huge difference between *Dream* and its two immediate predecessors is not only deeply significant but is, in fact, a basic difference between *Dream* and all of Shakespeare's great plays. From *Romeo* to *The Tempest,* they are each dominated and shaped by one lead role (Portia, Hal, Hamlet, Macbeth, Lear, Henry V, Brutus), sometimes by two (Hotspur, Falstaff, Othello and Iago, Anthony).

It would be hard to overstate the dramatic consequences of a play with nine lead roles (or with none). If the audience cannot focus on one or, usually, on at most two lead roles, how can spectator attention and plot continuity be maintained? How, indeed, can a playwright satisfactorily characterize nine lead roles in the same evening's work? He has only two and a half or three hours with which to operate. Divide 150 or 180 minutes by 9 and, even if there were no other characters present on stage, and no more or less wordless action to consume additional stage time, there would still be from 15 to a maximum of 20 minutes for each lead role. *Dream* is not a brief playlet, a mere interlude, but a full-length, five-act performance. It is plainly a vastly superior and a gorgeously satisfying performance vehicle. But how is that possible? No beef stew worth eating can be prepared with nine potatoes, a carrot, and a hamburger, nor can a functional football team be made up of nine centers, a pass thrower, and a pass catcher. What legerdemain, what the-hand-is-quicker-than-the-eye magic, has Shakespeare employed?

Under "Characterization," this first of my three subheadings, let me consider, in summary fashion rather than by close examination, only the three royal figures in *Dream,* a human duke and a fairy king and queen. To begin with the characters of highest social standing would be a proper Elizabethan approach—and I want to postpone textual analysis for the second and the third of my categories, "Narrative and Structure" and "Language."

Neither Theseus nor Oberon commands the stage as do Richard II and Bolingbroke, who have greater visibility—many more lines to speak, much more time in which to display themselves. Yet both Theseus and Oberon have the distinctly individuated personalities associated with lead roles. Theseus is quietly, confidently commanding. He is not arrogant, though understandably proud of his link with Hercules. (Who would not be?) For an Elizabethan male, he is remarkably deferential to his soon-to-be duchess. He is suave and sensitive in handling Egeus and the young lovers, not playing out his cards until he needs to, carefully conducting delicate negotiations in private. Though clearly well disposed toward a union between Lysander and Hermia, he does not make such a marriage possible, over the continued, stubborn objections of her father, until Demetrius' pursuit of Hermia has been terminally aborted. He is well inclined toward the artisans and their play, displaying tact and (for the time) a wonderfully sympathetic stance toward men considered to be infinitely below him. He is wise about the workings of the artistic mind. And all these traits are manifested in relatively spare, subtly eloquent ways, not even deeply expansive when he expounds on his all-pervading fascination—shared by Hippolyta, his Amazon queen—with the very sounds of *the* aristocratic avocation of the Renaissance, hunting.

Oberon is a totally different sort of ruler. His status as a fairy is not a controlling cause of his personality, except perhaps in his comparative immaturity: after all, fairies have no great need to grow up, or to be socially responsible. Oberon is inclined to arrogance, petulance, and the kind of slack but peremptory attitude

toward subordinates that he plainly shares with most human
rulers. He demands obedience without ensuring it. And when
he is opposed, he immediately seeks vengeance: neither concilia-
tion nor compromise ever occurs to him. He is capable of feeling
pity for Titania, wallowing in her ridiculous, drug-induced love
for Bottom—but only once she has agreed to give him the servant he so wants. Before that point, his almost adolescent relish for
her ludicrous displays is utterly shameless. He can think logically
and correctly about his status, as fairy and as a king, but has no patience for thought and reason in other contexts. Oberon is without question kingly—and because he for the most part acts in
ways that we, the audience, either approve of or find appropriate
to a fairy ruler, he does not present himself as obnoxious.

Titania is both a woman and, within her queenly provinces, a
ruler. Queens were notoriously subordinate to kings, in direct
confrontation, but capable of successful maneuvering in their
own best interests. Women, in Elizabethan perspective, were
more feeling toward others, especially other women. Women
were also viewed as sexually less self-controlled than men. These
characteristics are quite evident in Titania. But there is a good
deal more to her personality. She exudes fairy lightness, in movement, speech, and all her dealings. Oberon has compelled her into
her ludicrous relationship with Bottom, but like a hypnotist he
cannot eliminate her basic character: she perfectly understands
Bottom's unending talkativeness, and when she has him brought
to her bower, for sexual activity, she orders her servants to muzzle
him.. "Tie up my lover's tongue," she instructs, "bring him
silently" (3.1.180). Her impudent chiding of Oberon is wonderfully pert; her deft manipulation of Bottom is wholly admirable;
her re-emergence as a fully empowered queen is sweepingly

effected. Oberon is to tell her, she declares in her final lines, "How it came this night / That I sleeping here was found / With these mortals on the ground" (4.1.99–101). With these "mortals," indeed!

Shakespeare's "magic," in matters of characterization, is founded in (1) his amazing capacity for such three-dimensional, individuated portrayals, and (2) the narrative and structural urgencies that simultaneously link and shape such portrayals. *Dream* is a reciprocally integrated whole, a flowing series of evolving inter-relationships. Nothing—or very nearly nothing—is presented to us outside that evolution, which is constantly in motion. That is, nothing is presented in isolation, or purely for the sake of being inserted into the play. No songs are sung for the sake of having music; no words are spoken in order to make the drama eloquent; no actions are taken because action for the sake of action seems to the playwright to be necessary. *Dream* is a fully realized, totally interdependent entity—the kind of functioning, delicate complexity so perfectly engineered that it does not seem to be anything like as complex as in truly is, but merely light and "purely playful."

This is, of course, an exceedingly rare achievement, within the grasp of very, very few writers. In a university course dealing with sixteenth-century English lyric poetry, I once brought students through the marshes, bogs, underbrush, and half-cleared woodlands of Skelton, Surrey, Wyatt et al., up to the towering summit of Shakespeare's sonnets. Starting with the first sonnet, not particularly famous, I said that, without embroidering, I would show how many poetic balls this magician could and did keep in the air at the same time, effortlessly, seamlessly, unobtrusively. An hour later, I had still not exhausted *what was actually there,* and had to leave the remainder of this one uncelebrated poem for our next meeting.

Shakespeare is entirely human; he can and does make mistakes, he is capable of work that is less than completely, seamlessly perfect. But he is also an astonishing genius, an immortal mortal of a kind seldom seen on this earth. The rest of us inevitably have difficulty fully recognizing just what a towering figure like Shakespeare has given us. We ignore or, Lord help us, condescend to his achievement only at our own risk.

Narrative and Structure

The four-sided relationships between and among Lysander, Hermia, Demetrius, and Helena are the most obvious and, at the same time, the most complex narrative skeins from which Shakespeare weaves his play. The positions at the start are as follows:

1. Lysander loves Hermia
2. Demetrius loves Hermia
3. Hermia loves Lysander
4. Helena loves Demetrius

But the complications are immediately under way:

2a. Egeus, Hermia's father, wants her to marry Demetrius
3a. Theseus, ruling Duke of Athens, is obliged to endorse Egeus' right to have Hermia marry the man he wishes her to marry—and when Egeus invokes the terms of that law, requiring Hermia to marry her father's choice or become a nun or die, things turn distinctly dark
1a. Lysander and Hermia agree to meet in the wood outside Athens, and to elope
4a. Helena, Hermia's old friend, passes this information on to Demetrius

2b. Demetrius pursues the lovers, and Helena follows
Demetrius

It is night, it is dark, and it is Midsummer Night's Eve, known
also as St. John's Eve. This is the evening before the summer sol-
stice, an important seasonal event, observed all across Europe from
prehistorical times, and with great fervor and special rites. Matters
of love were of marked importance; supernatural beings were
thought to be especially evident; and though we have lost sight
(and knowledge) of much that was thought to take place, on that
night, neither Shakespeare nor his time had yet forgotten. And
more than likely, Shakespeare elaborated, and for artistic purposes
freely crossed one tradition with another.

Accordingly, after many exchanges between and among the
four lovers, Shakespeare introduces a major narrative intervention:

5. At Oberon's instigation, and in an attempt to improve
matters, Puck (mistaking one Athenian for another)
causes:
1b. Lysander to fall in love with Helena
1c. Demetrius to fall in love with Hermia

This in turn causes all manner of complications, progressing
through a swift-moving variety of circumstances to:

2c. Demetrius and Lysander developing serious hostility
toward each other, and
3c. Hermia and Helena following suit

Ultimately, Puck makes things well, and:

1. Lysander again loves Hermia
2. Hermia still loves Lysander

INTRODUCTION

3. Demetrius again loves Helena (to whom he had earlier been engaged)
4. Helena still loves Demetrius

which allows Theseus to override Egeus' objections, and three marriages are celebrated at once.

As thus schematicized, it surely sounds distinctly light, supremely playful. But this is no more than the plot, and narrative movement cannot be considered apart from dramatic structure. Narrative is in a sense more or less an outline, a skeleton; dramatic structure puts flesh on the bare bones. And Shakespeare builds that structure swiftly, yet subtly. Within fewer than a hundred lines, in the play's first scene, Egeus goes from a ranting father to a drastically threatening one; Theseus goes from celebratory prospective groom to stern authoritarian ruler, with whom Hermia tries, in vain, to dispute. "I would my father looked but with my eyes," she says. "Rather," Theseus declares, quietly switching the argument from emotions (hers) to morality (the law's), "your eyes must with [your father's] judgment look" (1.1.57–58). Theseus most delicately attempts to persuade her, first, to marry as she has been told to, but if not, then at least to live—and the play has just as delicately moved away from sheer narrative and into all the possible but as yet unknown complications of structure. Hermia declares, as emphatically as she can, that she will not marry Demetrius. Acting as a wise ruler, but also as a man now somehow personally involved in the lovers' situation, Theseus counsels her to "Take time to pause" (1.1.84). Lysander now adds another complication, revealing that Demetrius had earlier wooed Helena. At once, Theseus steps into even deeper possible structural depths:

I must confess that I have heard so much,
And with Demetrius thought to have spoke thereof.
But being over full of self affairs,
My mind did lose it. But, Demetrius, come,
And come, Egeus: you shall go with me.
I have some private schooling for you both. (1.1.111–16)

Shakespeare moves so fast, and with such a light step, that we can easily overlook the startling implications of these three and a half lines:

1. The supreme figure in Athens knows who has been wooing whom
2. It seems not to be generally understood that Theseus has his sources of information ("I have heard")
3. Theseus is (why?) apologetic ("I must confess")
4. More: he intended to speak to Demetrius about this (to say what?)
5. Theseus almost deferentially, and very indirectly, mentions the cause of his inaction, namely, his imminent wedding, "self affairs" of which he has been "over full" (what is the *real* reason for this strange self-criticism? to what does it connect? and where might it lead?)
6. "My mind did lose it" is cast as an extension of self-criticism—that is, negatively, but it is in fact a declaration that Theseus' mind/attention has now *found* the matter, and a muffled but plain assertion that this time he will not let it slip away

These are structural rather than purely narrative factors, because they are as yet inchoate, narratively unrealized. They are possibilities, motivating forces that *might* move the narrative this way, or perhaps that, if the other thing (whatever it is) does not intervene. If we speak of narrative as having threads, we must categorize dramatic structure in terms of implications, which may or may not turn into clear storyline threads.

Dream is so chock-full of dramatic structure (as simple, light narratives cannot be, by definition: that which is light cannot be dense) that, although Theseus seems to turn away, at this point, Shakespeare has still more motivational arrows in his quiver.

1. "You shall go with me," Theseus says—not to Lysander, not to Hermia, but to Egeus and Demetrius. "I have some private schooling for you both" ("schooling" is at least as pregnant, here, as "private": the meaning of the word— "scolding"—clearly depends on the fact that Elizabethan teachers were more corrective than persuasive).

2. After reaffirming her situation to Hermia, Theseus plants perhaps the most delicate bit of dramatic structure yet: it is "the law of Athens [which] yields you up," he says. In whose hands does that actually lie? His. But he separates himself from the law and adds, apparently to reinforce his own helplessness in the face of the law, "Which by no means we may extenuate." This is the first mention of extenuation, and it comes from Authority's own mouth. Much later, Theseus *will* extenuate the law. But here is where the seed of that has been planted.

Nor does Shakespeare allow lightness to interfere with the somber darkness he has created. Instead, as in truth he does over and over in *Dream,* he deepens the darkness that has fallen on Hermia. Lysander remarks on her pallor; she, apparently weeping, comments on her readily understandable sorrow. And Lysander launches into a commentary and illustration of the theme that "The course of true love never did run smooth" (1.1.134). They both wax eloquently and even passionately miserable, and we listen (or read) with troubled sympathy, knowing "how quick bright things come to confusion" (1.1.149).

The possibility of hope is only then broached. Not the certainty, but the possibility. Even Lysander, who suggests the scheme of fleeing from Athens, under cover of darkness, is not certain: "Keep promise, love," he urges (1.1.179). *We* may expect Hermia to be as good as her word, but he is plainly not quite sure. And at this point, as Lysander puts it, "Look, here comes Helena" (1.1.179)—and with her, inevitably, a quiver-full of structural complications. After Helena's dismal statement of her own love problems, and acting out of sympathy and affection for an old friend, Hermia assures Helena that Demetrius won't be seeing her again, because she and Lysander are eloping. Hermia and then Lysander leave— and Helena proceeds to open several Pandora boxes:

1. She's as pretty as Hermia: what's wrong?
2. Love itself is at fault, since "in choice he is so oft beguiled"
3. Until Demetrius "looked on Hermia's eyne," everything was fine
4. Though she clearly knows she ought not to, Helena resolves to inform Demetrius of Lysander and Hermia's plans; like a spy (the key word being "intelligence"), she knows she will be paid, though not very much, for her report (the key words being "dear expense" and "enrich"). She does not care what her betrayal might mean, since she

will at least "have his sight thither and back again" (1.1.251). Not only "is Love said to be a child," we might observe, but lovers too are like selfish little children. Indeed, much of the play is devoted to demonstrating exactly that, often quite devastatingly. But lightly?

Language

It is a truism that poetry, and especially non-narrative poetry, relies far more on the resources of sheer language than do drama and prose fiction. *Dream* is written, like much of Shakespeare's work, in both prose and verse, and it places heavy reliance on both characterization and narrative and dramatic structure. But all analytical categorizations are in a sense artificial devices, employed to clarify complex entities not readily amenable to analysis. In the end, we must remind ourselves that separation of any living entity into its component parts is precisely like dissection—and the dissecting knife either kills what is already dead, or is not picked up until death has taken place.

I have left examination of *Dream*'s language to the end of this introductory essay in order to emphasize how intimately, *essentially* it is interwoven with the play's characterizations and narrative and dramatic structure. Much of the verbal glory of *Dream,* inevitably, shines out of the poetry, a good deal of that poetry being not only in rhyme but in formal measures. But the prose, too, rises glowingly to the occasion:

I have had a most rare vision. I have had a dream, past the wit of man to say what dream it was. Man is but an ass, if he go about to expound this dream. Methought I was—

there is no man can tell what. Methought I was—and
methought I had—but man is but a patch'd fool, if he
will offer to say what methought I had. The eye of man
hath not heard, the ear of man hath not seen, man's hand
is not able to taste, his tongue to conceive, nor his heart
to report, what my dream was. (4.1.203–212)

This is Bottom speaking, as he wakens from his personal dream.
He remains the "bully Bottom" he has been from the start, bub-
bling over, grandiose. Shakespeare does not, like many play-
wrights then and now, switch his characters this way and that, first
good, then bad, depending on the dramatic needs of his play. But
Bottom's dream is—as we have witnessed him experiencing it—
too much for an untrained, unlearned, deeply plebian mind to
encompass. Bottom fairly stutters as he reaches for words, beginning to soar and then confounded by his stark inability to go far-
ther. He pauses, regroups, and does the same thing over and over.
It is marvelously in character; it is wonderfully fulfilling of the
narrative and the quivering, resonant depths of dramatic structure. But it is also masterfully glorious use of language, harnessing
words and their movement across the syntactical shape of wick-
edly pungent sentences. Having just emerged from the highest
point his life has ever known, or probably will ever know, Bottom
here achieves the closest thing to eloquence he will ever come to.
Yet there is no sophistication to his words, no reliance on the kind
of rhetorical devices, or the deft poetry, the loftier characters quite
naturally employ. It is all—like the porridge that Goldilocks finally tastes, and eats—*just right*. Quite rightly, Shakespeare never
assigns Bottom the sort of elaborately fanciful oration we hear
from Titania:

These are the forgeries of jealousy.
And never, since the middle summer's spring
Met we on hill, in dale, forest or mead,
By pavèd fountain or by rushy brook,
Or in the beachèd margent of the sea,
To dance our ringlets to the whistling wind,
But with thy brawls thou hast disturbed our sport.
Therefore the winds, piping to us in vain,
As in revenge have sucked up from the sea
Contagious fogs which, falling in the land,
Have every pelting river made so proud
That they have overborne their continents.
The ox hath therefore stretched his yoke in vain,
The ploughman lost his sweat, and the green corn
Hath rotted ere his youth attained a beard.
The fold stands empty in the drownèd field,
And crows are fatted with the murrion flock.
The nine men's morris is filled up with mud,
And the quaint mazes in the wanton green
For lack of tread are undistinguishable.
The human mortals want their winter cheer.
No night is now with hymn or carol blest.
Therefore the moon, the governess of floods,
Pale in her anger, washes all the air
That rheumatic diseases do abound.
And thorough this distemperature we see
The seasons alter. Hoary-headed frosts
Fall in the fresh lap of the crimson rose,
And on old Hiems' thin and icy crown
An odorous chaplet of sweet summer buds

Is, as in mockery, set. The spring, the summer,
The childing autumn, angry winter, change
Their wonted liveries. And the mazèd world,
By their increase, now knows not which is which.
And this same progeny of evils comes
From our debate, from our dissension.
We are their parents and original. (2.1.81–117)

What Titania is saying is that, just as she and Oberon have been
upset, so too has the world. They are immortal, but the consequences of their wrangling are everywhere visible and, for the
poor mortals who do not live in the fairies' shadow realm, those
consequences are exceedingly bad. I have summed up that "message" in a bare two sentences: Why does Titania require thirty-six
packed lines?

1. Titania is a queen; she will by her very nature negotiate—
   especially with the king who happens to be her husband—
   on the very highest level, taking the most commanding
   view possible.
2. The audience must be drawn into, made to deeply feel
   and to appropriately weigh the role of the fairies in this
   narrative. Fairy power must take on, for us, an importance
   that a merely "playful" drama cannot possess. Titania's long
   speech is elegant, to be sure, and singularly beautiful. Yet its
   resonance with the dramatic complexities of *Dream,* and
   especially its throbbing evocation of humankind's eternally
   precarious position in the physical universe, are every bit as
   important as the magnificently sweeping lines. Shakespeare's
   audience lived far more closely tied to the earth than do
   most of us, in the twenty-first century. Their response to

Titania's declarations were likely to be a good deal more
intense even than ours.

In this introductory essay, I have said and intend to say little
about Shakespeare's handling of the four young lovers' love ago-
nies. These miseries are real and not at all difficult to find. They
ought not to be perceived as either light or playful. There is
comedy in some of their encounters, notably those between
Demetrius and Lysander, but not much comedy in a desperate
Demetrius threatening Helena with his sword, or a terrified Hermia, left alone in the dark wood, running after her ever-faithful
Lysander—who stuns her with scorn and insults. All the lovers
are threatened with deprivation, desertion, bewildering confusion, betrayal, and even death. We do indeed know, this play being
a comedy and its ending assuredly happy, that everything will
come out well. But what we *feel,* as the lovers indeed feel while
experiencing their various torments, should be, and I think is, less
sanguine and often distinctly painful.

Let me conclude with Puck. Known also as Robin Goodfellow, he was in popular legend not always kind, and often rather
malicious. He was in fact not so much a fairy (the categories fade
into one another) as a goblin, and goblins were notoriously unpleasant. Shakespeare somewhat softens Puck's image—but not
entirely:

> I am that merry wanderer of the night.
> I jest to Oberon and make him smile
> When I a fat and bean-fed horse beguile,
> Neighing in likeness of a filly foal,
> And sometime lurk I in a gossip's bowl
> In very likeness of a roasted crab,

And when she drinks, against her lips I bob,
And on her withered dewlap pour the ale.
The wisest aunt, telling the saddest tale,
Sometime for three-foot stool mistaketh me.
Then slip I from her bum, down topples she,
And "tailor" cries, and falls into a cough,
And then the whole quire hold their hips and loffe,
And waxen in their mirth and neeze and swear
A merrier hour was never wasted there. (2.1.43 – 57)

Puck is, in a sense, the fairy-realm counterpart of Bottom: lively, forceful, self-absorbed, and rather crude. He is Oberon's jester, and does his job, on the whole, very well—though like Bottom he is demonstrably not infallible. Ariel, in *The Tempest,* is indeed a light-spirited fairy, but Puck has more than a little of the earthly about him. His roots are in the peasant wit of Chaucer's *Canterbury Tales,* not the fastidious tracery-work of Sir Philip Sidney, much less the elaborate Platonisms of Edmund Spenser's *Faerie Queen*.

For all that, Shakespeare gives Puck deftly turned, flowing, immaculately rhymed iambic pentameter couplets. This is perfectly polished verse, yet so tuned to who Puck is, and is not, that reading (and even hearing) this speech, most of us will not notice either the rhyming or even the iambic pentameter prosody. Art that does not seem artful: this is the fuel that *Dream*'s smooth, powerful engines run on. No one, not even Shakespeare, has ever written a more perfect, or more perfectly human, comedy.

SOME ESSENTIALS OF THE
SHAKESPEAREAN STAGE

The Stage

- There was no *scenery* (backdrops, flats, and so on).

- There were virtually no *on-stage props,* only an occasional chair or table, a cup or flask.

- *Costumes* (which belonged to and were provided by the individual actors) were very elaborate. As in most premodern and very hierarchical societies, clothing was the distinctive mark of who and what a person was.

- What the actors *spoke,* accordingly, contained both the dramatic and narrative material we have come to expect in a theater (or movie house) and (a) the setting, including details of the time of day, the weather, and so on, and (b) the occasion. The *dramaturgy* is thus very different from that of our own time, requiring much more attention to verbal and gestural matters. Strict realism was neither intended nor, under the circumstances, possible.

- There was *no curtain*. Actors entered and left via the side of the stage.

- In *public* theaters, there was no *lighting;* performances could take place only in daylight hours.

- For *private* theaters, located in large halls of aristocratic houses, candlelight illumination was possible.

The Actors

- Actors worked in *professional* for-profit companies, sometimes organized and owned by other actors, and sometimes by entrepreneurs who could afford to erect or rent the company's building. Public theaters could hold, on average, a probable two-thousand-size audience, most of whom viewed and listened while standing. Significant profits could be and were made. Private theaters were smaller, more exclusive; profit-making was not an issue.

- There was *no stage director.* A prompter, presumably standing in one wing, had a text marked with entrances and exits; a few of these survive. Rehearsals seem to have been largely group affairs; we know next to nothing of the dynamics involved or from what sort of texts individual actors worked. However, we do know that, probably because Shakespeare's England was largely an oral culture, actors learned their parts rapidly and retained them intact for years. This was *repertory* theater, regularly repeating popular plays and introducing some new ones each year.

- *Women* were not permitted on the professional stage. All female parts were acted by prepubescent *boys.*

The Audience

- London's professional theater operated in what might be called a "red-light" district, featuring brothels, restaurants, and the kind of *open-air entertainment* then most popular, like bear-baiting (in which a bear, tied to a stake, was set on by dogs).

- A theater audience, like most of the population of Shakespeare's England, was largely made up of *illiterates.* Being able to read and write, however, had nothing to do with intelligence or concern with language, narrative, and characterization. People attracted to the theater tended to be both extremely verbal and extremely volatile. Actors were sometimes attacked, when the audience was dissatisfied; quarrels and fights were relatively common. Women were commonly in attendance, though no reliable statistics exist.

- Plays were almost never *printed,* during Shakespeare's lifetime. Not only did drama not have the cultural esteem it has in our time, but neither did literature in general. Shakespeare wrote a good deal of nondramatic poetry yet so far as we know did not authorize or supervise whatever of his work appeared in print during his lifetime.

- Playgoers, who had paid good money to see and hear, plainly gave dramatic performances very careful, detailed attention. For some closer examination of such matters, see Burton Raffel, "Who Heard the Rhymes and How: Shakespeare's Dramaturgical Signals," *Oral Tradition* 11 (October 1996): 190–221, and Raffel, "Metrical Dramaturgy in Shakespeare's Earlier Plays," *CEA Critic* 57 (Spring–Summer 1995): 51–65.

A Midsummer Night's Dream

CHARACTERS (DRAMATIS PERSONAE)

Theseus (Duke of Athens)
Egeus (Hermia's father)
Lysander (courtier in love with Hermia)
Demetrius (courtier in love with Hermia)
Philostrate (Theseus' Master of the Revels)
Lords / Attendants

Peter Quince (carpenter: "Prologue")
Snug (woodworker:[1] "Lion")
Nick Bottom (weaver: "Pyramus")
Francis Flute (bellows mender: "Thisbe")
Tom Snout (tinker:[2] "Wall")
Robin Starveling (tailor: "Moonshine")

Hippolyta (Queen of the Amazons)
Hermia (in love with Lysander)
Helena (in love with Demetrius)

Oberon (Fairy King)
Titania (Fairy Queen)
Puck / Robin Goodfellow (Oberon's jester)
Peaseblossom (Titania's fairy)
Cobweb (Titania's fairy)
Moth (Titania's fairy)
Mustardseed (Titania's fairy)
Other Fairies

1 also called a "joiner"
2 a mender of metal utensils

Act I

Theseus' palace, Athens

ENTER THESEUS, HIPPOLYTA, PHILOSTRATE,
AND ATTENDANTS

Theseus Now fair[3] Hippolyta, our nuptial hour[4]
    Draws on apace.[5] Four happy days[6] bring in
    Another moon.[7] But O, methinks,[8] how slow
    This old moon wanes![9] She lingers[10] my desires,

3 beautiful (often used conventionally, politely)★
4 our nuptial hour = time of our wedding
5 draws on apace = comes about/advances quickly/speedily
6 four happy days = the length of the enormously important Midsummer
   festival (Midsummer being a time for lovers, for all manner of magic, and for
   unconventional or mad behavior)
7 (the play is "a night's dream"; the moon is goddess of the night – and in
   Shakespeare's time moon and stars were far more visible and of very much
   greater cultural importance)
8 it seems to me★
9 decreases, dwindles
10 dawdles over, delays

5   Like to a stepdame[11] or a dowager[12]
       Long withering out[13] a young man's revenue.[14]

Hippolyta Four days will quickly steep[15] themselves in night,
       Four nights will quickly dream away the time,
       And then the moon, like to a silver bow

10   New bent in heaven,[16] shall behold the night
       Of our solemnities.[17]

Theseus   Go, Philostrate,
       Stir up[18] the Athenian youth to merriments,
       Awake the pert and nimble[19] spirit of mirth,
       Turn melancholy forth[20] to funerals.

15   The pale companion[21] is not for our pomp.[22]

EXIT PHILOSTRATE

       Hippolyta, I wooed thee with my sword,[23]
       And won thy love, doing thee injuries.
       But I will wed thee in another key,
       With pomp, with triumph and with reveling.

11 stepmother
12 widow with inherited property (which a son who marries will have in her
   stead)
13 withering out = drying out, shriveling
14 income
15 soak, saturate
16 (the new or crescent moon, pale/silver in color, is slender and curved like a
   bow; eternally chaste Diana, Apollo's twin, is a nature, a hunting, and a moon
   goddess)
17 ceremonies, celebrations
18 stir up = move, urge, stimulate, excite
19 pert and nimble = lively/quick/cheerful and clever/swift/light/agile
20 away
21 pale companion = timorous/pallid associate/partner/fellow★
22 magnificent show/celebration★
23 (Theseus, an ally of Hercules, had defeated her in battle; in some versions
   Theseus rapes her, and in others she is killed by Hercules)

ENTER EGEUS, HERMIA, LYSANDER, AND DEMETRIUS

Egeus	Happy be Theseus, our renownèd Duke!	20

Theseus Thanks, good[24] Egeus.[25] What's the news with thee?

Egeus   Full of vexation[26] come I, with complaint

Against my child, my daughter Hermia.[27]

Stand forth,[28] Demetrius.[29] My noble lord,

This man hath my consent to marry her.   25

Stand forth, Lysander.[30] And, my gracious Duke,

This man hath bewitched the bosom[31] of my child – [32]

Thou, thou, Lysander, thou hast given her rhymes,[33]

And interchanged[34] love tokens[35] with my child.

Thou hast by moonlight at her window sung,   30

With feigning[36] voice, verses of feigning love,

And stol'n[37] the impression[38] of her fantasy[39]

With bracelets[40] of thy hair, rings, gawds,[41] conceits,[42]

24 (form of conventional polite address)★
25 IYdjis
26 trouble, distress, grief
27 HERmiyA
28 step forward
29 diMItriyUS
30 liSANder
31 heart★
32 this MAN hath beWITCHED the BOSom OF my CHILD
33 poems, verses
34 exchanged
35 gifts
36 deceitful, artful
37 appropriated/taken possession of/captured secretly/dishonestly/by trickery
38 belief
39 imagination★ (and STOL'N the imPRESsion OF her FANtaSY)
40 ornamental bands
41 showy ornaments, gewgaws
42 fancy trifles

Knacks,[43] trifles, nosegays,[44] sweetmeats[45] – messengers[46]
35 Of strong prevailment[47] in unhardened[48] youth.
With cunning hast thou filched[49] my daughter's heart,
Turned her obedience, which is due to me,
To stubborn harshness. And, my gracious Duke,
Be it so[50] she will not here before[51] your Grace
40 Consent to marry with Demetrius,
I beg the ancient privilege[52] of Athens.
As she is mine, I may dispose[53] of her,
Which shall be either to this gentleman
Or to her death, according to our law,
45 Immediately[54] provided in that case.

Theseus What say you, Hermia? Be advised, fair maid.
To you your father should be as a god,
One that composed[55] your beauties, yea, and one
To whom you are but as a form in wax,
50 By him imprinted,[56] and within his power
To leave[57] the figure[58] or disfigure[59] it.

43 trinkets
44 bouquets
45 cookies, cakes, and other sweet, candylike delights
46 envoys, ambassadors, forerunners
47 influence
48 still soft/inexperienced
49 stolen (not from herself but from her father, to whom its destiny was owed)
50 be it so = if it happens/comes to pass that
51 in front of★
52 legal right
53 do with, deliver
54 directly (without pause or appeal)
55 produced, formed
56 stamped, shaped
57 allow to remain
58 form, shape
59 destroy, deface

Demetrius is a worthy[60] gentleman.

Hermia   So is Lysander.

Theseus   In himself he is.

But in this kind,[61] wanting[62] your father's voice,[63]

The other[64] must be held[65] the worthier.   55

Hermia   I would[66] my father looked but[67] with my eyes.

Theseus   Rather your eyes must with his judgment look.

Hermia   I do entreat your Grace to pardon[68] me.

I know not by what power[69] I am made bold,[70]

Nor how it may concern[71] my modesty[72]   60

In such a presence[73] here to plead my thoughts.

But I beseech your Grace that I may know

The worst that may befall[74] me in this case,

If I refuse to wed Demetrius.

Theseus   Either to die the death, or to abjure,   65

For ever, the society of men.[75]

Therefore, fair Hermia, question your desires,

60 honorable, reputable★
61 character, function★
62 lacking★
63 approval, agreement
64 man (Demetrius)
65 accepted, considered★
66 wish★
67 only
68 make allowance for, excuse
69 capacity, strength, authority, permission
70 daring, presumptuous, immodest★
71 effect, implicate
72 obligatory womanly behavior/reserve★
73 a presence = company
74 happen/occur to★
75 (not the society of *males* but – she being forced to become a nun – the society of all other human beings)

ACT I • SCENE I

Know of[76] your youth, examine well your blood,[77]

Whether, if you yield not to your father's choice,

70 You can endure the livery[78] of a nun,

For aye[79] to be in shady cloister[80] mewed,[81]

To live a barren sister[82] all your life,

Chanting faint[83] hymns to the cold fruitless[84] moon.

Thrice blessèd they that master so[85] their blood

75 To undergo[86] such maiden pilgrimage.[87]

But earthlier happy[88] is the rose distilled[89]

Than that, which withering on the virgin thorn,[90]

Grows, lives, and dies in single[91] blessedness.[92]

Hermia So will I grow, so live, so die, my lord,

80 Ere[93] I will yield my virgin patent[94] up

Unto his lordship,[95] whose unwishèd[96] yoke[97]

76 know of = be aware of
77 emotions, passions★
78 garments, clothing★ ("habit")
79 ever★
80 shady cloister = retired/sheltered convent/nunnery/religious habitat
81 confined, cooped up
82 nun
83 feeble, timid, languid
84 cold fruitless = lacking ardor/warmth/sexless barren/childless
85 master so = overcome/tame in that way
86 to undergo = in order to experience/endure/subject themselves to
87 maiden pilgrimage = virginal★ religious journey
88 earthlier happy = happier on earth
89 concentrated/purified into scent/perfume by the process of distillation
90 aversion/hostility/prickliness (to men)
91 solitary, celibate; slight, poor, trivial
92 (the religious reward available to either sex for remaining sexless)
93 before, sooner than★
94 title, privilege
95 his lordship = Demetrius' control/rule/mastery (lord = husband)★
96 whose unwishèd = to whose unwanted
97 wooden collar on an animal's neck, to link it with another animal★

My soul consents not to give sovereignty.

Theseus Take time to pause and, by the next new moon –
The sealing[98] day betwixt[99] my love and me,
For everlasting bond[100] of fellowship[101] –   85
Upon that day either prepare to die
For disobedience to your father's will,
Or else to wed Demetrius, as he[102] would,
Or on Diana's altar to protest[103]
For aye austerity[104] and single life.   90

Demetrius Relent, sweet Hermia. And Lysander, yield
Thy crazèd title[105] to my certain[106] right.

Lysander   You have her father's love, Demetrius.
Let me have Hermia's. Do[107] you marry him.[108]

Egeus   Scornful Lysander! True, he hath my love,   95
And what is mine[109] my love shall render[110] him.
And she is mine, and all my right[111] of her
I do estate[112] unto Demetrius.

---

98 (to put a seal on something is to make it visibly genuine / approved)
99 between
100 mutually binding responsibilities
101 partnership, sharing
102 that is, Egeus
103 formally declare, solemnly affirm
104 life that is harsh, rigorous, severe ("ascetic")
105 crazèd title = flawed/unsound claim (as in title to land or other property,
    the man possesses the woman)
106 reliable, trustworthy, settled★
107 proceed to ("go ahead and")★
108 let ME have HERMya's DO you MARry HIM
109 (Hermia)
110 give, deliver, hand over, surrender to
111 moral and legal entitlement
112 (verb) give, bestow

Lysander I am, my lord, as well derived[113] as he,
100   As well possessed.[114] My love is more[115] than his,
My fortunes[116] every way as fairly ranked,[117]
If not with vantage,[118] as Demetrius'.
And, which is more than all these boasts can be,
I am beloved of beauteous Hermia.
105   Why should not I then prosecute[119] my right?
Demetrius, I'll avouch[120] it to his head,[121]
Made love[122] to Nedar's daughter, Helena,
And won her soul. And she, sweet lady, dotes,[123]
Devoutly dotes, dotes in idolatry,
110   Upon this spotted[124] and inconstant man.
Theseus I must confess that I have heard so much,
And with Demetrius thought to have spoke thereof.
But being over full[125] of self[126] affairs,
My mind did lose[127] it. But, Demetrius, come,
115   And come, Egeus: you shall[128] go with me.

113 descended
114 having property/wealth
115 greater
116 standing, hopes
117 strong, great
118 if not with vantage = and perhaps advantageously
119 pursue, persist in, take advantage of
120 certify, prove, confirm, guarantee
121 to his head = to his face, to him directly
122 made love = wooed, courted
123 to be wildly/foolishly in love★
124 morally stained/blemished
125 preoccupied, absorbed
126 my own
127 forget, failed to keep track/sight of
128 (1) expression of future tense ("will"), (2) expression of obligation
("must")★

I have some private schooling[129] for you both.
For you, fair Hermia, look you arm[130] yourself
To fit your fancies[131] to your father's will,
Or else the law of Athens yields[132] you up –
Which by no means we may extenuate[133] –   120
To death, or to a vow of single life.
Come,[134] my Hippolyta: what cheer,[135] my love?
Demetrius and Egeus, go along,[136]
I must employ[137] you in some business[138]
Against[139] our nuptial, and confer with you   125
Of something nearly that[140] concerns yourselves.

Egeus   With duty[141] and desire[142] we follow you.

EXEUNT ALL BUT LYSANDER AND HERMIA

Lysander How now,[143] my love? Why is your cheek so pale?
How chance[144] the roses there do fade so fast?

Hermia   Belike[145] for want of rain, which I could well   130

129 scolding
130 provide/furnish with the means
131 moods, inclinations
132 gives, delivers
133 mitigate, lessen
134 (an expression of encouragement, unrelated to the usual meanings of
    "come")
135 what cheer = how are you, how do you feel
136 go along = come with/follow me
137 make use of
138 BIziNESS
139 with regard to★
140 nearly that = that particularly/especially
141 submission, respect★
142 pleasure, satisfaction
143 how now = how do you do, how are you (conventional polite greeting)
144 does it happen, come about
145 probably, possibly, perhaps★

      Beteem[146] them from the tempest[147] of my eyes.

Lysander Ay me![148] For aught[149] that I could ever read,

      Could ever hear by tale[150] or history,[151]

      The course[152] of true[153] love never did run smooth,

135   But either it[154] was different[155] in blood[156] –

Hermia O cross![157] Too high to be enthralled[158] to low.[159]

Lysander Or else misgraffèd[160] in respect of years[161] –

Hermia O spite![162] Too old to be engaged[163] to young.

Lysander Or else it stood[164] upon the choice of friends –

140 Hermia O hell! To choose love by[165] another's eyes.

Lysander Or if there were a sympathy[166] in choice,

      War, death, or sickness did lay siege to it,

      Making it momentany[167] as a sound,

146 pour on
147 violent commotion/disturbance
148 ay me = oh/ah me
149 anything
150 talk, conversation
151 narrative, story
152 path★
153 steadfast, constant, faithful, sincere★
154 the love relationship
155 DIfeRENT
156 descent, lineage, family
157 affliction, misfortune
158 enslaved
159 one of the parties is too exalted in rank/descent to be bound to someone
    so low in rank/descent
160 badly matched
161 age
162 outrage, insult★
163 entangled, attached
164 it stood = the projected marriage rested/existed
165 under/because of the decisions/supervision of
166 affinity, attraction, harmony, concord
167 transitory, evanescent, momentary (MOmenTAny)

Swift as a shadow, short as any dream,

Brief as the lightning in the collied[168] night   145

That, in a spleen,[169] unfolds[170] both heaven and earth,

And ere a man hath power to say "Behold!"

The jaws of darkness do devour it up.

So quick bright[171] things come to confusion.[172]

Hermia   If then true lovers have been ever crossed,[173]   150

It stands as an edict[174] in destiny.

Then let us teach our trial[175] patience,[176]

Because it is a customary[177] cross,

As due[178] to love as thoughts and dreams and sighs,

Wishes and tears, poor[179] fancy's followers.   155

Lysander   A good persuasion.[180] Therefore hear me, Hermia.

I have a widow aunt, a dowager

Of great revenue,[181] and she hath no child.

168 darkened, murky
169 impulse, whim, caprice, fit of temper
170 displays, lays open (to sight)
171 quick bright = quickly/lively shining/gleaming
172 ruin, destruction (conFYUziON)*
173 ever crossed = always/eternally (adverb) thwarted/afflicted
174 rule, law (eeDICT)
175 testing, struggle, affliction
176 PAseeENCE
177 common, usual
178 as due = just as rightful/owed/belonging
179 poor fancy's = humble/insignificant* imagination's
180 argument, conviction, opinion
181 reVENue (*A Dictionary of the English Language,* ed. Samuel Johnson
    [London: William Ball, 1838], p. 998, col. 1, gives the pronunciation
    reVENue, and *An English Pronouncing Dictionary,* 10th ed., ed. Daniel Jones
    [London: Dent, 1949], p. 363, col. 1, gives the same pronunciation as a
    secondary choice, "chiefly heard in legal and parliamentary circles"; note
    that the word is spelled in the First Quarto reuennew, and, in assorted other
    surviving documents, revennewe, reuenine, reuenew, renue, revenos (pl.),
    reuenue, revennue, revenuz (pl), reuenewse (pl), revenewed)

From Athens is her house remote[182] seven leagues.[183]
160 And she respects[184] me as her only son.
There, gentle[185] Hermia, may I marry thee.
And to that place the sharp[186] Athenian law
Cannot pursue us. If thou lov'st me then,[187]
Steal forth[188] thy father's house tomorrow night.
165 And in the wood, a league without[189] the town,
Where I did meet thee once with Helena
To do observance[190] to a morn of May,
There will I stay[191] for thee.

Hermia   My good Lysander,
I swear to thee, by Cupid's strongest bow,
170 By his best arrow with the golden head,
By the simplicity[192] of Venus' doves,[193]
By that which knitteth[194] souls and prospers[195] loves,
And by that fire which burned the Carthage queen[196]
When the false Troyan[197] under sail was seen,
175 By all the vows that ever men have broke,

182 distant, far
183 (1 league = approx. 3 mi.)
184 regards, considers, treats
185 well born★
186 severe, harsh, merciless
187 therefore
188 from, out of★
189 outside
190 customary ritual/worship
191 wait★
192 innocence, sincerity, straightforwardness
193 (the goddess' carriage was drawn by sacred doves)
194 fastens, attaches, joins
195 causes to flourish/succeed
196 (Dido)
197 (Aeneas, her lover, who was deserting her)

In number more than ever women spoke,
In that same place thou hast appointed[198] me,
Tomorrow truly[199] will I meet with thee.
Lysander Keep promise,[200] love. Look, here comes Helena.

Hermia   God speed,[201] fair Helena. Whither away?[202]   180
Helena   Call you me fair? That fair again unsay.
Demetrius loves your fair. O happy fair!
Your eyes are lode stars,[203] and your tongue's sweet air[204]
More tuneable[205] than lark to[206] shepherd's ear
When wheat is green, when hawthorn buds appear.   185
Sickness[207] is catching. O were favor[208] so,
Yours would I catch,[209] fair Hermia, ere I go.
My ear should [210] catch your voice, my eye your eye,
My tongue should catch your tongue's sweet melody.
Were the world mine, Demetrius being bated,[211]   190
The rest I'd give to be to you translated.[212]

198 fixed/arranged/prescribed/decreed for
199 faithfully, trustworthily★
200 your promise
201 God speed = may God make things be well with you (a conventionally
     polite greeting or farewell)
202 are you going
203 lode stars = stars that show the way
204 breath, voice
205 melodious, harmonious, sweet-sounding
206 to a
207 (here, the sickness is love distress)
208 liking, preference★
209 (First Quarto: Your words I catch; Second Folio (1632): Your words I'd
     catch; "yours would" is a common editorial emendation)
210 would
211 taken away, subtracted
212 conveyed, transferred

O teach me how you look,[213] and with what art[214]

You sway[215] the motion of Demetrius' heart.

Hermia I frown upon him, yet he loves me still.[216]

195 *Helena* O that[217] your frowns would teach my smiles such skill![218]

Hermia I give him curses,[219] yet he gives me love.

Helena O that my prayers could such affection move!

Hermia The more I hate, the more he follows me.

Helena The more I love, the more he hateth me.

200 *Hermia* His folly, Helena, is no fault of mine.

Helena None but your beauty. Would that fault were mine.

Hermia Take comfort: he no more shall see my face.

Lysander and myself will fly[220] this place.

Before the time I did Lysander see,

205 Seemed Athens as[221] a paradise to me.

O then what graces[222] in my love do dwell,

That he hath turned a heaven unto a hell.

Lysander Helen, to you our minds we will unfold.

Tomorrow night, when Phoebe[223] doth behold

210 Her silver visage[224] in the wat'ry glass,[225]

---

213 use your eyes
214 skill, artifice, craft
215 swerve, move, affect
216 always, constantly (adverb)★
217 if only
218 capability, cleverness, knowledge, understanding
219 negative comments (curse: then meant primarily invocations to or against the/a deity)
220 hurry from, flee★
221 like
222 charms, pleasing qualities★
223 (Diana, the moon goddess)
224 face★
225 mirror

Decking[226] with liquid pearl the bladed[227] grass –
A time that lovers' flights doth still conceal –
Through Athens' gates have we devised to steal.[228]

Hermia　And in the wood, where often you and I
Upon faint[229] primrose beds[230] were wont[231] to lie,　　　　215
Emptying our bosoms of their counsel[232] sweet,[233]
There my Lysander and myself shall meet,
And thence from Athens turn away our eyes,
To seek new friends and stranger companies.[234]
Farewell, sweet playfellow.[235] Pray thou for us.　　　　220
And good luck grant thee thy Demetrius.
Keep word,[236] Lysander. We must starve our sight
From lovers' food till morrow deep midnight.[237]

Lysander　I will, my Hermia.

EXIT HERMIA

Helena, adieu.

As you on him, Demetrius dote[238] on you.　　　　225

EXIT LYSANDER

226 covering, clothing (verb)★
227 having many blades
228 devised to steal = planned/determined★ to go secretly
229 pale (the primrose bears pale blossoms)
230 (1) sleeping/resting place, (2) plant/flower beds
231 accustomed, in the habit★
232 exchange of opinions/plans/intentions/secrets★
233 (First Quarto: swelled)
234 stranger companies = the society/companionship of strangers (stranger,
　　here, is closer to an adjective than to a noun; First Quarto: strange
　　companions)
235 companion
236 (in line 000, Lysander similarly tells her to keep her promise)
237 morrow deep midnight = tomorrow at solemn/important midnight (deep
　　can also mean very late after)
238 may Demetrius be wildly/foolishly in love with

Helena How happy some o'er[239] other some[240] can be!

Through Athens I am thought as fair as she.

But what of that? Demetrius thinks not so.

He will not know[241] what all but[242] he do know,

230   And as he errs, doting on Hermia's eyes,

So[243] I, admiring of[244] his qualities.[245]

Things base and vile,[246] holding no quantity,[247]

Love can transpose[248] to form and dignity.[249]

Love looks not with the eyes, but with the mind.

235   And therefore is wing'd Cupid painted[250] blind.

Nor hath Love's mind of any judgment taste:[251]

Wings, and no eyes, figure unheedy[252] haste.

And therefore is Love said to be a child,

Because in choice he is so oft beguiled.

240   As waggish[253] boys in game[254] themselves forswear,[255]

So the boy, Love, is perjured[256] everywhere.

239 more than (o'er: over)
240 some . . . some = some people . . . other people
241 will not know = (1) refuses/does not want to know, (2) (future tense)
242 except
243 so do
244 admiring of = wondering/marveling at
245 character, nature
246 base and vile = of little value and little appreciated/paltry
247 holding no quantity = (1) having/containing no duration, (2) out of proportion
248 change, transform, convert
249 form and dignity = beauty and worth/excellence/honor
250 painted blind = represented in drawings/paintings as being blind
251 a sense/feeling
252 figure unheedy = portray/represent inattentive/reckless
253 mischievous
254 sport, fun, amusement★
255 themselves forswear = tell lies, swear falsely (themselves: here a reflexive syntactical marker)
256 breaks oaths, commits perjury

For ere Demetrius looked on Hermia's eyne,
He hailed[257] down oaths that he was only mine.
And when this hail some heat[258] from[259] Hermia felt,
So he dissolved,[260] and showers of oaths did melt.   245
I will go tell him of fair Hermia's flight.
Then to the wood will he tomorrow night
Pursue her, and for this intelligence[261]
If I have thanks, it is[262] a dear[263] expense.
But herein mean[264] I to enrich[265] my pain,   250
To have his sight[266] thither and back again.

EXIT

257 poured, threw
258 fervor, ardor, passion
259 because of
260 melted
261 information (especially as conveyed by spies)
262 will be for him
263 dear expense = precious/lavish/strenuous/difficult disbursement
264 propose, intend
265 improve
266 his sight = the sight of him

SCENE 2

Athens. Quince's house

ENTER QUINCE, SNUG, BOTTOM, FLUTE,
SNOUT, AND STARVELING

Quince Is all our company[1] here?

Bottom You were best to call them generally,[2] man by man,
according to the scrip.[3]

Quince Here is the scroll[4] of every man's name, which is thought
5   fit, through all Athens, to play in our interlude[5] before the
Duke and the Duchess, on his wedding day at night.

Bottom First, good Peter Quince, say what the play treats on,[6]
then read the names of the actors, and so grow to a point.[7]

Quince Marry,[8] our play is, "The most lamentable[9] comedy, and
10   most cruel death of Pyramus and Thisbe."

Bottom A very good piece of work, I assure you, and a merry.
Now, good Peter Quince, call forth your actors by the scroll.
Masters,[10] spread yourselves.[11]

---

1 fellowship, companionship★
2 individually (Bottom mangles the word "severally")
3 piece of paper
4 list, roll
5 (once descriptive of a between-acts humorous playlet – or mime
performance – by Shakespeare's time the word was used for popular
comedies, and at some point for stage drama generally)★
6 treats on = deals with
7 grow to a point = come to a conclusion? a definite position? (the workmen-
actors do not invariably speak with verbal precision)
8 an exclamation (originally an oath employing the Virgin Mary's name)★
9 (1) mournful, (2) deplorable, pitiable, wretchedly bad
10 workmen qualified to be in business for themselves
11 make yourselves known

Quince Answer as I call you. Nick Bottom, the weaver.

Bottom Ready. Name what part I am for,[12] and proceed.   15

Quince You, Nick Bottom, are set down[13] for Pyramus.

Bottom What is[14] Pyramus? A lover, or a tyrant?

Quince A lover, that kills himself most gallant[15] for love.

Bottom That will ask[16] some tears in the true performing of it. If
    I do it, let the audience look to[17] their eyes. I will move[18]   20
    storms, I will condole[19] in some measure.[20] To[21] the rest –
    yet my chief humor[22] is for a tyrant. I could play Ercles[23]
    rarely,[24] or a part to tear a cat[25] in, to make all split.[26]
    (*he declaims*)

         The raging[27] rocks   25
         And shivering shocks[28]
      - Shall break the locks
            Of prison gates,

12 representing
13 set down = put / written down ("scheduled," on the list from which Quince
    is reading)
14 what is = what is the nature / condition of
15 splendid, grand, courtier-like
16 call for
17 look to = attend to, take care / be careful of
18 start, bring, stir up, excite
19 lament, grieve
20 in some measure = somewhat, to an extent, in some degree
21 for, as for
22 disposition, temperament, style, liking
23 Hercules (mangled – though not Cockney-fashion, since "the correct use of
    h had not yet become a shibboleth of gentility"; Kökeritz, *Shakespeare's
    Pronunciation,* 308)
24 unusually well, splendidly
25 tear a cat = swagger, rant
26 all split = the whole audience go to pieces (see *OED,* tear, 1d, illustration)
27 violent
28 sudden violent collisions / blows

And Phibbus' car[29]

30   Shall shine from far

And make and mar[30]

The foolish Fates.

This was lofty.[31] Now name the rest of the players. This is
Ercles' vein,[32] a tyrant's vein. A lover is more condoling.[33]

35   *Quince*   Francis Flute, the bellows mender.

Flute   Here, Peter Quince.

Quince   Flute, you must take Thisbe on you.[34]

Flute   What is Thisbe? A wandering knight?[35]

Quince   It is the lady that Pyramus must[36] love.

40   *Flute*   Nay, faith, let me not play a woman. I have a beard
coming.[37]

Quince   That's all one.[38] You shall play it in a mask, and you may
speak as small[39] as you will.

Bottom   An[40] I may hide my face, let me play Thisbe, too. I'll

45   speak in a monstrous little voice:
"Thisne, Thisne."[41]

---

29 Phibbus' car = the chariot of Phoebus Apollo, the sun god
30 make and mar = create/cause total success or total failure ("make or break")
31 exalted, sublime
32 strain, style
33 comforting, sympathetic
34 take . . . on = perform, undertake, tackle
35 wandering knight = knight errant (errant = roaming, traveling)
36 is supposed/needs/ought/is fated to
37 (since Flute is a master workman, he cannot be a budding adolescent and
must, accordingly, be for some reason testosterone-deficient)
38 all one = one and the same ("irrelevant")
39 gently, soft
40 if★
41 (misprint for Thisbe? pet name of Thisbe?)

"Ah, Pyramus, my lover dear! Thy Thisbe dear, and lady dear!"

Quince   No, no. You must play Pyramus, and Flute, you Thisbe.

Bottom   Well, proceed.   50

Quince   Robin Starveling, the tailor.

Starveling Here, Peter Quince.

Quince   Robin Starveling, you must play Thisbe's mother.[42] Tom Snout, the tinker.

Snout   Here, Peter Quince.   55

Quince   You, Pyramus' father.[43] Myself, Thisbe's father. Snug, the joiner, you the lion's part. And I hope here is a play fitted.[44]

Snug   Have you the lion's part written? Pray you, if it be, give it me, for I am slow of study.[45]   60

Quince   You may do it extempore,[46] for it is nothing but roaring.

Bottom   Let me play the lion, too. I will roar, that[47] I will do any man's heart good to hear me. I will roar, that I will make the Duke say, "Let him roar again, let him roar again."   65

Quince   An you should do it too terribly, you would fright the Duchess and the ladies, that they would shriek. And that were enough to hang us all.[48]

---

42 (the mother does not have any part in the play)
43 you, Pyramus' father = and you must play Pyramus' father
44 proper, appropriate
45 of study = (1) reading, learning, (2) memorizing
46 without preparation, offhand
47 so that
48 (hang us all: to offend lordly persons could be sufficient cause for execution)

All   That would hang us, every mother's son.[49]

70   *Bottom*   I grant you, friends, if you should fright the ladies out of
their wits,[50] they would have no more discretion[51] but to
hang us. But I will aggravate[52] my voice so that I will roar
you[53] as gently as any sucking[54] dove. I will roar you an
'twere[55] any nightingale.

75   *Quince*   You can play no part but Pyramus. For Pyramus is a
sweet-faced man, a proper man as[56] one shall see in a
summer's day, a most lovely[57] gentleman-like man. Therefore
you must needs[58] play Pyramus.

Bottom   Well, I will undertake it. What beard[59] were I best to
80   play it in?

Quince   Why, what you will.

Bottom   I will discharge[60] it in either your[61] straw color beard,
your orange tawny[62] beard, your purple in grain[63] beard, or
your French crown color[64] beard, your perfect[65] yellow.

---

49 every mother's son = each and all
50 causing the ladies to faint (the five wits = the five senses)
51 freedom of decision
52 (aggravate = magnify, worsen; Bottom uses aggravate instead of moderate or mitigate)
53 ("you" is syntactically meaningless in modern English, as here used)
54 fledgling, baby
55 an 'twere = as if it were
56 a proper man as = as proper (excellent, fine, admirable) a man as
57 loving, affectionate
58 of necessity
59 (false/artificial beard, held in place by string)
60 perform, speak
61 (your, repeated four times, is in modern English syntactically meaningless)
62 brown
63 in grain = dyed in grain/fast color dye
64 crown color = the color of a king's golden crown
65 full, deep

Quince Some of your French crowns[66] have no hair[67] at all, and   85
    then you will play barefaced.[68] But[69] masters, here are your
    parts, and I am to[70] entreat you, request you and desire you,
    to con[71] them by tomorrow night, and meet me in the palace
    wood, a mile without the town, by moonlight. There will we
    rehearse. For if we meet in the city, we shall be dogged[72] with   90
    company,[73] and our devices[74] known. In the meantime, I will
    draw[75] a bill of properties,[76] such as our play wants.[77] I pray
    you, fail me not.

Bottom We will meet, and there we may rehearse most
    obscenely[78] and courageously.[79] Take pains,[80] be perfect.[81]   95
    Adieu.

66 a gold coin (but see note 68 on a possibly different meaning intended, here,
    for "crown")
67 color? (that is, they are not in fact gold, and thus not yellow, as Bottom has
    just said they were?)
68 (literally, with a bare face, but the word also means shameless, audacious,
    impudent, which would be consistent with the anti-French sentiment
    of "French crowns [that] have no hair"; it is also possible, and has been
    suggested, that Quince means "crown" as heads, referring to the English-
    alleged prevalence of syphilitic baldness among Frenchmen: syphilis was
    called the French pox, in England, and in France was known as the English
    pox)
69 in any case (that is, aside from any discussion of colors)
70 I am to = it is my task to
71 know/learn
72 followed, pursued, haunted, hounded
73 an assemblage/collection/multitude of people
74 purposes, intentions, plans*
75 compile, write
76 bill of properties = memorandum of needed things (costumes, furniture,
    etc.)
77 requires, needs
78 (Bottom-mangling of something like seemly: properly, decorously, suitably)
79 fearlessly, boldly
80 take pains = work hard, take the trouble
81 be perfect = know your part perfectly

Quince At the Duke's oak we meet.
Bottom Enough. Hold or cut bowstrings.[82]

EXEUNT

---

82 hold or cut bowstrings = stick to/stay with/continue it ("hold fast") or else give it up ("fish or cut bait")

Act 2

SCENE I

A wood near Athens

Enter, from opposite sides, a Fairy, and Puck

Puck   How now, spirit! Whither wander you?

Fairy   Over hill, over dale,[1]
　　　Thorough[2] bush, thorough brier,
　　Over park,[3] over pale,[4]
　　　Thorough flood,[5] thorough fire.[6]　　　　　　　5
　　I do wander everywhere,
　　Swifter than the moon's sphere.[7]
　　And I serve the fairy queen,

1 valley (not yet the poeticized word it has become)
2 THOrough
3 enclosed woodland
4 fence
5 water, stream
6 (used broadly, as one of the four elements: earth, air, water, fire)
7 the transparent globe enclosing all planetary bodies, including stars, in
　Ptolemaic astronomy (SWIFTer THAN the MOON'S SPHERE: the
　pronunciation of moon can be lengthened, but it is not bisyllabic)

To dew[8] her orbs[9] upon the green.[10]
10   The cowslips[11] tall her pensioners[12] be,
In their gold coats spots you see.[13]
Those be rubies, fairy favors.[14]
In those freckles live[15] their savors.[16]
I must go seek some dewdrops here,
15   And hang a pearl[17] in every cowslip's ear.

Farewell, thou lob[18] of spirits. I'll be gone.
Our queen and all our elves come here anon.[19]
Puck The king[20] doth keep his revels[21] here tonight.
Take heed[22] the queen come not within his sight.
20   For Oberon is passing fell[23] and wrath[24]
Because that she as her attendant hath[25]
A lovely boy, stol'n from an Indian king.

8 moisten with dew
9 circles ("fairy rings")
10 (1) plot of grass, (2) vegetation, verdure, greenery★
11 yellow flowers
12 (1) gentlemen at arms, royal bodyguards serving in the palace,
    (2) mercenaries, bodyguards
13 in THEIR gold COATS SPOTS you SEE
14 gifts★
15 are found, exist
16 scent, perfume
17 (that is, a dewdrop – rounded and glistening like a pearl)
18 country bumpkin, clown, lout ("lump")
19 soon, directly, in a short while★
20 (that is, king of the fairies: Oberon)
21 keep his revels = hold/celebrate his merrymaking/feast
22 take heed = be careful
23 passing fell = exceedingly/surpassingly★ angry/enraged
24 resentful, angry ("wroth")
25 because that she as her attendant hath = because she has as her servant

She never had so sweet a changeling.[26]
And jealous Oberon would have the child
Knight[27] of his train,[28] to trace[29] the forests wild.[30]   25
But she perforce[31] withholds the lovèd boy,
Crowns him with flowers and makes him all her joy.
And now they[32] never meet in grove[33] or green,
By[34] fountain clear, or spangled[35] starlight sheen,[36]
But they do square,[37] that[38] all their elves for fear   30
Creep into acorn cups[39] and hide them[40] there.
Fairy Either I mistake[41] your shape and making[42] quite,[43]
      Or else you are that shrewd and knavish[44] sprite[45]
      Called Robin Goodfellow.[46] Are not you he[47]

26 child stolen by fairies (ordinarily, but not here, the ugly child the fairies substitute for the one stolen)
27 servant boy
28 retainers, attendants★
29 tread, travel, traverse
30 not domesticated or cultivated
31 by force (French *par force*), of necessity★
32 Oberon and Titania
33 (1) walks/avenues in a forest, (2) a small woodland★
34 near, beside★
35 spangle = round bits of metal, perforated for attaching to clothing, etc.; stars were referred to as spangles
36 brightness, gleaming
37 they never meet ... but they square = every time they meet ... they quarrel/fall out ("square off")
38 so that
39 hollow acorn shells
40 themselves
41 (verb) am wrong about
42 shape and making = appearance/look★ and form/build
43 completely, entirely
44 shrewd and knavish = malicious/mischievous★ and roguish/rascally
45 spirit★
46 goodfellow = (1) reveler, convivial companion, (2) thief
47 called RObin GOOD felLOW are NOT you HE

35   That frights the maidens[48] of the villagery,[49]

Skim[50] milk, and sometimes labor[51] in the quern,[52]

And[53] bootless[54] make the breathless[55] housewife churn,[56]

And sometime make the drink[57] to bear no barm,[58]

Mislead night wanderers,[59] laughing at their harm?[60]

40   Those that Hobgoblin[61] call you, and sweet Puck,[62]

You do their work, and they shall have good luck.

Are not you he?

Puck   Thou speak'st aright,[63]

---

48 maiden = young unmarried woman/girl

49 villages generally

50 you who skim . . . labor . . . make . . . make . . . mislead

51 (*OED,* labor, verb, 3, identifies the specific meanings rubbing, pounding, beating)

52 grinding apparatus, hand mill (exactly what mischief Puck creates in the quern is not clear, but the word is exclusively pronounced KWERN: the word churn is exclusively pronounced TCHURN; there is no *OED* identification of these two words, and there are many combinations – for example, quernmill, quernstone – conclusively identifying quern as a hand mill/grinding apparatus)

53 and also (further separating what Puck "labors" at and what he "makes," the First Quarto has a comma after quern)

54 unsuccessfully, uselessly, futilely (*OED,* bootless, 4, identifies such quasi-adverbial usages)

55 panting

56 labor at churning (verb: women work at churning, not at the churn per se)

57 alcoholic beverage (usually beer, which was made at home)

58 foam, froth (produced by and indicative of yeast-impelled fermentation; since the verb is bear – support, carry – barm cannot here mean, as has been suggested, either the yeast itself or its working)

59 WANdrers

60 injury, pain, distress

61 bog(e)y, terrifying apparition (Hob = familiar/rustic version of the names Robert and Robin)

62 (from about A.D. 1000 to 1500, puck/pouke was regarded as devilish; thereafter he mutated into the tricksy goblin/sprite known as Puck, Hobgoblin, or Robin Goodfellow)

63 correctly, justly

I am that merry wanderer of the night.
I jest to Oberon and make him smile
When I a fat and bean-fed[64] horse beguile,[65]   45
Neighing in likeness of[66] a filly[67] foal,
And sometime lurk I in a gossip's bowl[68]
In very[69] likeness of a roasted crab,[70]
And when she drinks, against her lips I bob,[71]
And on her withered dewlap[72] pour the ale.   50
The wisest aunt,[73] telling the saddest[74] tale,
Sometime for three-foot stool mistaketh me.
Then slip I from her bum,[75] down topples she,
And "tailor"[76] cries, and falls into a cough,
And then the whole quire[77] hold their hips and loffe,[78]   55
And waxen[79] in their mirth and neeze[80] and swear
A merrier hour was never wasted[81] there.

---

64 fat and bean-fed: fat because fed on beans in addition to/rather than straw/
  hay
65 divert, lead astray
66 in likeness of = like, in imitation of
67 young female horse
68 gossip's bowl = female tattler/spreader of tales' drinking vessel
69 true, real ("faithful")*
70 wild/crab apple
71 move jerkily up and down
72 withered dewlap = shriveled folds of flesh hanging from the neck
73 older woman
74 gravest, most serious/dignified
75 buttocks, rear end
76 (perhaps drawn from taylard, or the state of having a tail, and signifying here
  something like "O my tail"?)
77 church choir?
78 laugh (and THEN the WHOLE quire HOLD their HIPS and LOFFE)
79 increase
80 sneeze, snort
81 (1) spent, (2) squandered

But room,[82] fairy! Here comes Oberon.

Fairy   And here my mistress. Would that he[83] were gone!

ENTER, FROM ONE SIDE, OBERON, WITH HIS TRAIN,
AND FROM THE OTHER SIDE TITANIA, WITH HERS

60   *Oberon*   Ill[84] met by moonlight, proud[85] Titania.

Titania   What, jealous[86] Oberon? Fairies, skip hence.[87]

I have forsworn[88] his bed and company.

Oberon   Tarry, rash wanton.[89] Am not I thy lord?

Titania   Then I must be thy lady.[90] But I know

65   When[91] thou hast stol'n away from fairy land,

And in the shape of Corin[92] sat all day,

Playing on pipes[93] of corn[94] and versing[95] love

To amorous Phillida.[96] Why art thou here,

Come from the farthest steep[97] of India,

70   But[98] that, forsooth,[99] the bouncing[100] Amazon,[101]

82 make room, clear the way
83 Oberon
84 badly, wrongfully, hostilely
85 haughty, arrogant
86 (1) angry, wrathful, (2) covetous, envious, greedy, grudging
87 skip hence = hurry / leap away / at a distance
88 abandoned, renounced
89 tarry, rash wanton = wait,★ hasty / reckless / impetuous undisciplined /
   uncontrolled / rebellious★ one
90 lady love, woman to whom you owe chivalric devotion
91 the times when
92 (typical male name, in the pastoral tradition)
93 (any flutelike musical instrument)
94 grain stalk (in British usage, corn = wheat★)
95 reciting poems of / about
96 (typical female name, in the pastoral tradition)
97 heights, hills
98 except, for any reason other than
99 truly, in truth
100 ungainly (that is, masculine-like)
101 Hippolyta

Your buskined[102] mistress and your warrior love,
To Theseus must[103] be wedded, and you come
To give[104] their bed joy and prosperity.
Oberon How canst thou thus for shame, Titania,
Glance at[105] my credit[106] with Hippolyta,   75
Knowing I know thy love[107] to Theseus?
Didst thou not lead him through the glimmering[108] night
From Perigenia,[109] whom he ravishèd,
And make him with fair Aegle[110] break his faith
With Ariadne and Antiopa?[111]   80
Titania These are the forgeries of jealousy.
And[112] never, since the middle summer's spring[113]
Met we[114] on hill, in dale, forest or mead,[115]
By pavèd fountain[116] or by rushy brook,[117]
Or in the beachèd margent[118] of the sea,   85
To dance our ringlets[119] to the whistling wind,

102 wearing a kind of half-boot
103 is to be/going to be
104 bestow upon, grant
105 glance at = allude/refer to/hit at, in passing/obliquely
106 reputation, credibility, influence, trust
107 affectionate solicitude/tenderness/attachment
108 feebly/faintly/intermittently shining*
109 PERiDJEENya (daughter of a bandit killed by Theseus)
110 EEGle (a nymph)
111 with ARiyADne AND anTIYoPA (Ariadne = daughter of King Minos of
    Crete; Antiopa = princess of Boeotia)
112 and in addition
113 middle summer's spring = the starting/rising of midsummer
114 Titania and her followers
115 meadow
116 pavèd fountain = clear-flowing stream with a pebbly bed
117 rushy brook = brook lined/covered with rushes/reeds
118 beachèd margent = beached margin/edge
119 circular dance/fairy ring

But with thy brawls[120] thou hast disturbed our sport.[121]
Therefore the winds, piping[122] to us in vain,
As[123] in revenge have sucked up from the sea
90 Contagious fogs[124] which, falling in[125] the land,
Have every pelting[126] river made so proud
That they have overborne[127] their continents.[128]
The ox hath therefore stretched[129] his yoke in vain,
The ploughman lost[130] his sweat, and the green corn
95 Hath rotted ere his youth attained a beard.[131]
The fold[132] stands empty in the drownèd field,
And crows are fatted with the murrion flock.[133]
The nine men's morris[134] is filled up[135] with mud,
And the quaint mazes[136] in the wanton green
100 For lack of tread[137] are undistinguishable.[138]

120 quarrels, squabbles
121 amusement, entertainment★
122 whistling, playing (as on a flutelike instrument)
123 as if
124 contagious fogs = infectious/contagion-carrying thick mists/watery
    vapors
125 into, on
126 insignificant, petty, worthless
127 overcome ("overflowed")
128 containing agents, banks
129 strained to its full capacity
130 has wasted
131 attained a beard = grown/achieved/obtained its hairlike tufts
132 animal pen/enclosure
133 with the murrion flock = by/on the animals killed by pestilence/plague
    ("murrain")
134 positions cut in grass for a game played with pegs ("men")
135 filled up = covered over
136 quaint mazes = skilled/ingenious labyrinths
137 treading, footsteps
138 indistinct

The human mortals want their winter cheer.[139]
No night is now with hymn or carol[140] blest.
Therefore the moon, the governess of floods,[141]
Pale in her anger, washes[142] all the air
That[143] rheumatic[144] diseases do abound.   105
And thorough[145] this distemperature[146] we see
The seasons alter. Hoary-headed[147] frosts
Fall in the fresh lap[148] of the crimson rose,
And on old Hiems'[149] thin and icy crown[150]
An odorous chaplet[151] of sweet summer buds   110
Is, as in mockery, set. The spring, the summer,
The childing[152] autumn, angry winter, change
Their wonted[153] liveries. And the mazèd[154] world,
By their increase,[155] now knows not which is which.
And this same progeny[156] of evils comes   115

139 mirth, gaiety, joy (not all editors agree, but First Quarto "here" appears, in
    context, to be a printer's error)
140 joyous song
141 tides
142 bathes, wets, moistens
143 so that
144 watery secretions (RHEUmaTIC)
145 through, by means of (THOra)
146 derangement, disturbance, disordered condition, excess
147 white/gray topped
148 fresh lap = newly blossomed folds/flaps
149 winter's
150 thin and icy crown = spare/lean and ice-covered head
151 odorous chaplet = fragrant/scented wreath/garland
152 fertile, fruitful
153 usual/customary
154 bewildered, confused, dazed, terrified ("amazed")
155 their increase = the seasons' (1) increments/additions/augmentations/
    enlargements, (2) fruit/offspring
156 (1) descendants, offspring, children, issue, (2) results, outcome

From our debate,[157] from our dissension.[158]

We are their parents and original.[159]

Oberon Do you amend[160] it, then. It lies in[161] you.

Why should Titania cross[162] her Oberon?

120 I do but beg a little changeling boy

To be my henchman.[163]

Titania   Set your heart at rest:

The fairy land[164] buys not the child of[165] me.

His mother was a votress[166] of my order,[167]

And in the spicèd[168] Indian air, by night,

125 Full often hath she gossiped by my side,

And sat with me on Neptune's yellow sands,

Marking th'embarkèd traders[169] on the flood.[170]

When[171] we have laughed to see the sails conceive[172]

And grow big-bellied with the wanton[173] wind,

157 strife, quarreling

158 discord, disagreement (disSENsiON)

159 source, origin

160 correct, rectify, improve★

161 lies in = depends/rests on/upon

162 thwart, oppose

163 groom, page, squire

164 the fairy land = the whole/entire fairy land

165 from

166 person bound by a vow/oath to some group/form of worship

167 group, company, society

168 aromatic, fragrant

169 marking th'embarkèd traders = observing/noting the passing (just setting out? freighted?) trading ships/merchant vessels

170 water (though a newly embarked ship would usually be sailing on the tide)

171 on which occasions

172 become pregnant (that is, swell out as the wind blows)

173 lascivious (not as common as the word's other meanings, in Shakespeare's time, but cited as early as 1391 and found elsewhere in Shakespeare's work)

Which she, with pretty[174] and with swimming gait[175]   130
Following[176] – her womb then rich[177] with my
young squire –
Would imitate, and sail upon the land
To fetch me trifles, and return again
As[178] from a voyage, rich with merchandise.
But she, being mortal, of that boy did die,   135
And for her sake do I rear up her boy,
And for her sake I will not part with him.

Oberon How long within[179] this wood intend you stay?

Titania Perchance till after Theseus' wedding day.
If you will[180] patiently dance in our round,[181]   140
And see our moonlight revels, go with us.
If not, shun me, and I will spare[182] your haunts.

Oberon Give me that boy, and I will go with thee.

Titania Not for thy fairy kingdom. Fairies, away!
We shall chide downright,[183] if I longer stay.   145

EXIT TITANIA WITH HER TRAIN

Oberon Well, go thy way.[184] Thou shalt not from[185] this grove

174 clever, artful, ingenious, admirable, fine★
175 swimming gait = walking as easily/smoothly as if swimming
176 afterwards
177 great, large, ample
178 as if
179 inside★
180 wish to
181 round dance, circle★ (if YOU will PAtientLY dance IN our ROUND)
182 keep clear of ("refrain from visiting")
183 brawl/wrangle out and out/thoroughly
184 go thy way = go on your own road/path
185 have gone from (that is, he will act at once)

Till[186] I torment thee for this injury.[187]
My gentle Puck, come hither. Thou rememb'rest
Since once[188] I sat upon[189] a promontory,
150 And heard a mermaid on a dolphin's back
Uttering such dulcet[190] and harmonious breath[191]
That the rude[192] sea grew civil[193] at her song,
And certain[194] stars shot madly from their spheres,
To hear the sea-maid's music?

Puck   I remember.

155 *Oberon* That very time I saw, but thou couldst not,
Flying between the cold moon and the earth,[195]
Cupid all armed.[196] A certain[197] aim he took
At a fair vestal thronèd by the west,[198]
And loosed his love-shaft[199] smartly[200] from his bow
160 As it should[201] pierce a hundred thousand hearts.
But I might[202] see young Cupid's fiery[203] shaft

186 before
187 insult, affront★
188 when once
189 on
190 sweet, agreeable, soothing
191 sounds
192 barbarous, uncivilized, unmannerly★
193 orderly, refined, polite★
194 fixed
195 FLYing beTWEEN the COLD moon AND the EARTH
196 ready for "war," armored
197 precise, exact, unerring
198 fair vestal thronèd by the west = lovely virgin sitting on a western throne
    (that is, Queen Elizabeth I)
199 loosed his love-shaft = released his love-creating arrow
200 vigorously
201 as it should = as if it were to
202 could
203 glowing, flashing

Quenched[204] in the chaste[205] beams of the watery moon,
And the imperial votress passèd[206] on,[207]
In maiden meditation, fancy free.
Yet marked I where the bolt[208] of Cupid fell.   165
It fell upon a little western flower,
Before milk white, now purple with love's wound,
And maidens call it "love-in-idleness."[209]
Fetch me that flower. The herb I showed thee once.
The juice of it on sleeping eyelids laid   170
Will make or man or woman[210] madly dote
Upon the next live creature that it[211] sees.
Fetch me this herb, and be thou here again
Ere the leviathan[212] can swim a league.
Puck   I'll put a girdle[213] round about the earth   175
In forty minutes.

EXIT

Oberon   Having once[214] this juice,
I'll watch Titania when she is asleep,
And drop the liquor of it in her eyes.
The next thing then she, waking, looks upon,

204 extinguished
205 celibate, sexually pure, virtuous
206 proceeded
207 AND the imPERyalVOtress PASsed ON
208 projectile, arrow
209 pansies
210 or man or woman = either man or woman
211 the eye/the person
212 enormous sea animal of biblical mention, usually identified as the whale
    (leVAYaTHAN)
213 belt ("line")
214 having once = once I have

180   Be it on lion, bear, or wolf, or bull,

       On meddling[215] monkey, or on busy[216] ape,[217]

       She shall pursue it with the soul[218] of love.

       And ere I take this charm from off her sight,

       As I can take it with another herb,

185   I'll make her render up her page to me.

       But who comes here? I am invisible,

       And I will overhear their conference.

     ENTER DEMETRIUS, WITH HELENA FOLLOWING HIM

Demetrius I love thee not, therefore pursue me not.

       Where is Lysander and fair Hermia?

190   The one I'll slay, the other slayeth me.

       Thou told'st me they were stol'n unto this wood,

       And here am I, and wode[219] within this wood,

       Because I cannot meet my Hermia.

       Hence, get thee gone, and follow me no more.

195 *Helena*   You draw[220] me, you hard-hearted adamant.[221]

       But yet you draw not iron, for my heart

       Is true[222] as steel. Leave[223] you your power to draw,

       And I shall have no power to follow you.

Demetrius Do I entice you? Do I speak you fair?[224]

---

215 interfering
216 constantly in motion
217 (by Shakespeare's time, apes were known to be distinct from monkeys)
218 the soul = all the emotions / passions
219 insane
220 pull, lead, allure, attract (like a magnet)
221 mythical substance, hardest of anything known
222 firm, steadfast, reliable
223 relinquish, give up, abandon
224 (1) courteously, kindly, (2) beautifully, nobly

Or rather do I not in plainest truth   200
  Tell you I do not, nor I cannot love you?
Helena   And even, for that, do I love you the more.
  I am your spaniel.[225] And, Demetrius,
  The more you beat me, I will fawn on you.
  Use[226] me but as your spaniel, spurn me, strike me,   205
  Neglect me, lose me – only give me leave,
  Unworthy as I am, to follow you.
  What worser place can I beg in your love –
  And yet a place of high respect with me –
  Than to be usèd as you use your dog?   210
Demetrius Tempt not too much the hatred of my spirit,
  For I am sick when I do look on thee.
Helena   And I am sick when I look not on you.
Demetrius You do impeach[227] your modesty too much,
  To leave the city and commit yourself   215
  Into the hands of one that loves you not –
  To trust the opportunity[228] of night
  And the ill counsel[229] of a desert[230] place
  With the rich worth[231] of your virginity.
Helena   Your virtue is my privilege,[232] for that[233]   220
  It is not night when I do see your face.

225 cringing, fawning
226 treat*
227 hurt, harm, call into question, discredit
228 convenience/advantageousness for doing things
229 ill counsel = immoral/depraved/wicked plans/purposes/intentions/
    deliberations/secrets
230 lonely, uninhabited
231 value
232 immunity, special position/advantage, security
233 for that = because

Therefore I think I am not in the night,
Nor doth this wood lack worlds of company,
For you, in my respect,[234] are all the world.
225   Then how can it be said I am alone,
When all the world is here to look on me?
Demetrius   I'll run from thee and hide me in the brakes,[235]
And leave thee to the mercy of wild beasts.
Helena   The wildest[236] hath not such a heart as you.
230   Run when you will. The story shall be changed:[237]
Apollo flies,[238] and Daphne holds the chase;[239]
The dove[240] pursues the griffin;[241] the mild hind[242]
Makes speed to catch the tiger – bootless speed,
When cowardice pursues and valor flies.
235 *Demetrius*   I will not stay[243] thy questions. Let me go –
Or if thou follow me, do not believe
But I shall do thee mischief in the wood.
Helena   Ay, in the temple, in the town, the field,
You do me mischief. Fie, Demetrius.
240   Your wrongs do set a scandal on my sex.
We cannot fight for love, as men may do.
We should[244] be wooed and were not made to woo.

---

234 opinion, regard, esteem
235 bushes, bushwood, briers
236 wildest beast
237 shall be changed = must be transmuted/turned to something else
238 Apollo flies = Apollo, who had been pursuing Daphne, runs away/flees
239 Daphne (DAFnee, who had been running away) holds the chase = Daphne
    maintains/keeps up the pursuit
240 gentle innocent
241 mythical beast, with the head and wings of an eagle, the body and legs of a
    lion
242 mild hind = tame/gentle female deer
243 endure/wait for? stop?
244 ought to

EXIT DEMETRIUS

I'll follow thee and make a heaven of hell,
To die upon the hand I love so well.

EXIT HELENA

Oberon Fare thee well, nymph. Ere he do leave this grove,   245
Thou shalt fly him, and he shall seek thy love.

ENTER PUCK

Hast thou the flower there? Welcome, wanderer.
Puck   Ay, there it is.
Oberon   I pray thee, give it me.
I know a bank[245] where the wild thyme[246] blows,
Where oxlips[247] and the nodding violet grows,   250
Quite over-canopied[248] with luscious woodbine,[249]
With sweet musk roses[250] and with eglantine.[251]
There sleeps Titania sometime of the[252] night,
Lulled[253] in these flowers with dances and delight.
And there the snake throws[254] her enameled[255] skin,   255
Weed[256] wide enough to wrap a fairy in.[257]

245 raised/sloping ground★
246 herbal shrub with aromatic leaves
247 flowering herb, related to primrose and cowslip
248 over canopied = covered over
249 luscious woodbine = sweet/pleasant vine (Virginia creeper, honeysuckle)★
250 musk roses = rambling white-flowered roses
251 sweetbriar
252 of the = at
253 calmed, quieted
254 casts, discards
255 glossy, ornamented
256 article of clothing, garment
257 weed WIDE eNOUGH to WRAP a FAIry IN

And with the juice of this I'll streak[258] her eyes,
And make her full of hateful fantasies.[259]
Take thou some of it, and seek through this grove.[260]
260   A sweet Athenian lady is in love
With a disdainful[261] youth. Anoint[262] his eyes.
But do it when the next thing he espies[263]
May[264] be the lady. Thou shalt know the man
By the Athenian garments he hath on.
265   Effect[265] it with some care, that he may prove
More fond on[266] her than she upon[267] her love.[268]
And look[269] thou meet me ere the first cock crow.[270]
Puck Fear not, my lord, your servant shall do so.

EXEUNT

258 rub, smear
259 hateful fantasies = repulsive / obnoxious / odious★ hallucinations / mental
    images / figments of the imagination
260 take THOU some OF it AND seek THROUGH this GROVE (n.b.:
    prosodic scanning is often *not* the same as speaking / reading; there is an
    ongoing and important tension between the two approaches)
261 contemptuous, scornful
262 smear, rub
263 sees, perceives
264 can
265 accomplish, bring about★
266 fond on = infatuated with / foolishly in love★ with
267 of
268 her love = him
269 make sure, take care
270 (fairies practice white, as contrasted with black magic, being beneficent, not
    evil; but they too are subject to — albeit not quite so rigorously — the natural
    limits imposed on witches, demons, et al., and necessarily observe the basic,
    natural distinction between darkness and light, night and day)

SCENE 2

Another part of the wood

Titania Come, now a roundel[1] and a fairy song.
    Then for[2] the third part of a minute, hence,
    Some to kill cankers[3] in the musk rose buds,
    Some war with reremice[4] for their leathern[5] wings,[6]
    To make my small elves[7] coats, and some keep back[8]   5
    The clamorous[9] owl that nightly[10] hoots and wonders[11]
    At our quaint spirits.[12] Sing me now asleep.
    Then to[13] your offices[14] and let me rest.

    You spotted snakes with double[15] tongue,
    Thorny hedgehogs, be not seen,   10
    Newts and blind worms[16] do no wrong,

1 round dance
2 before
3 caterpillars
4 bats
5 leatherlike
6 some WAR with REriMICE for their LEAthern WINGS
7 small elves: fairies are shaped more or less like humans, but elves are dwarflike
8 keep back = restrain, hold back
9 noisy
10 every night
11 marvels, is astonished by
12 quaint spirits = (1) clever/ingenious, (2) unfamiliar/odd/curious songs (*OED,* spirit, 15d)
13 go and do
14 duties, responsibilities★
15 forked
16 reptiles, then confused with adders ("slow-worms")

Come not near our fairy queen.
    Philomel,[17] with melody
    Sing in our sweet lullaby,
15   Lulla, lulla, lullaby,[18] Lulla, lulla, lullaby,
    Never harm, nor[19] spell nor charm,[20]
    Come our lovely lady nigh.[21]
    So good night, with lullaby.

Weaving[22] spiders, come not here.
20   Hence, you long-legged spinners,[23] hence!
Beetles black approach not near.
Worm nor snail do no offense.[24]
    Philomel, with melody,
    Sing in our sweet lullaby,
25   Lulla, lulla, lullaby. Lulla, lulla, lullaby,
    Never harm, nor spell, nor charm,
    Come our lovely lady nigh.
    So goodnight, with lullaby.

Fairy   Hence, away! Now all is well.
30   One aloof[25] stand sentinel.

EXEUNT FAIRIES. TITANIA SLEEPS

17 the nightingale (FIloMEL)
18 LULaBEE
19 nor . . . nor = neither . . . nor
20 spell . . . charm = magic incantations
21 near
22 web making
23 spiders
24 harm, injury, damage
25 at some distance

ENTER OBERON AND SQUEEZES THE JUICE
ON TITANIA'S EYELIDS

Oberon   What thou see'st, when thou dost wake,[26]
  Do it[27] for thy true love take.
  Love and languish[28] for his sake.
  Be it[29] ounce,[30] or cat, or bear,
  Pard,[31] or boar with bristled hair,[32]   35
  In thy eye that[33] shall appear,
  When thou wak'st, it is thy dear.[34]
  Wake, when some vile[35] thing is near.

EXIT

ENTER LYSANDER AND HERMIA

Lysander Fair love, you faint[36] with wand'ring in the wood,
  And to speak troth,[37] I have forgot our way.[38]   40
  We'll rest us, Hermia, if you think it good,
  And tarry for the comfort of the day.

26 WHAT thou SEE'ST, when THOU dost WAKE (songs usually use lines of
    shorter metrical length)
27 whatever you see
28 droop, pine
29 be it = whether it is
30 lynx (and other small feline animals)
31 leopard, panther
32 bristled hair = hair that is stiff, prickly, rough
33 in thy eye that shall appear = whatever you see
34 darling, dear one
35 disgusting, base, despicable, repulsive
36 lose heart, grow weak (verb)
37 truth
38 path, road

Hermia   Be it so, Lysander. Find you out[39] a bed,[40]

For I upon this bank will rest my head.

45 *Lysander*   One turf[41] shall serve as pillow for us both:

One heart, one bed, two bosoms[42] and one troth.[43]

Hermia   Nay, good Lysander. For my sake, my dear,

Lie further off yet,[44] do not lie so near.

Lysander   O take the sense,[45] sweet, of my innocence.[46]

50 Love takes[47] the meaning, in love's conference.[48]

I mean that my heart unto yours is knit,[49]

So that but one heart we can make of it.

Two bosoms interchainèd[50] with an oath.

So then two bosoms and a single troth.[51]

55 Then by your side no bed-room me deny.

For lying so, Hermia, I do not lie.[52]

Hermia   Lysander riddles[53] very prettily.

Now much beshrew my manners, and my pride,[54]

---

39 find you out = locate/obtain yourself
40 be it SO lySANDer FIND you OUT a BED
41 bit of grassy ground
42 breast (of both men and women: neither bosom nor breast then referred
  only to women)
43 (the word's basic meaning, truth, is here extended to cover an agreement/
  pledge to marry)
44 further off yet = still further off
45 take the sense = understand the meaning
46 moral purity
47 captures, seizes, gains possession of
48 speech, talk, discourse
49 knotted, fastened together★
50 linked
51 (here, too, the word's basic meaning is extended to faith/trust)
52 speak a falsehood
53 speaks enigmatically/puzzlingly ("in riddles," here in puns)
54 much beshrew my manners and my pride = hang (a ladylike version of
  "damn")★ my behavior and self-esteem

If Hermia meant to say Lysander lied.
But, gentle friend, for love and courtesy   60
Lie further off, in human modesty.[55]
Such separation as may well be said
Becomes a virtuous bachelor, and a maid,
So far be distant, and good night, sweet friend.
Thy love ne'er alter till thy sweet life end.   65

Lysander Amen, amen, to that fair prayer, say I,
And then end life when I end loyalty![56]
Here is my bed. Sleep give thee all his rest.

Hermia   With half[57] that wish the[58] wisher's eyes be pressed.

THEY SLEEP

ENTER PUCK

Puck   Through the forest have I gone,   70
But Athenian[59] found I none
On whose eyes I might approve[60]
This flower's force[61] in stirring[62] love.
Night and silence. – Who is here?
Weeds of Athens he doth wear.   75
This is he, my master said,
Despised[63] the Athenian maid.

---

55 human modesty = humanly proper self-control/reserve/deferential feelings
56 faithfulness to one's word
57 (that is, the "all" should be divided into two equal parts, one half for each of them)
58 let/may the
59 ATHenIYan
60 demonstrate
61 strength, power★
62 stirring up (verb)
63 scorned, looked down on★

And here the maiden, sleeping sound,
On the dank[64] and dirty ground.
80 Pretty soul, she durst not lie
Near this lack-love, this kill-courtesy.[65]
Churl,[66] upon thy eyes I throw
All the power this charm doth owe.[67]
When thou wak'st, let love forbid
85 Sleep his seat[68] on thy eyelid.
So[69] awake, when I am gone,
For I must now to Oberon.

EXIT

ENTER DEMETRIUS AND HELENA, RUNNING

Helena   Stay, though thou kill me, sweet Demetrius.
Demetrius I charge[70] thee, hence! And do not haunt me[71] thus.
90 *Helena*   O wilt thou darkling[72] leave me? Do not so.
Demetrius Stay, on thy peril.[73] I alone[74] will go.

EXIT

Helena   O, I am out of breath in this fond[75] chase:

64 damp, wet
65 kill-courtesy = boor, lout (NEAR this LACKlove THIS kill COURteSY)
66 peasant, rustic, base fellow
67 own, possess
68 forbid sleep his seat = command sleep to give up his place (that is, Lysander will not be able to sleep, because of love)
69 thus
70 command, order
71 haunt me = run after/be so much around me
72 in darkness
73 on thy peril = at your risk
74 by myself
75 infatuated, foolish

The more my prayer,[76] the lesser is my grace.[77]
Happy is Hermia, wheresoe'er she lies,
For she hath blessèd[78] and attractive[79] eyes.   95
How came her eyes so bright? Not with salt tears:
If so, my eyes are oftener washed than hers.
No, no. I am as ugly as a bear,
For beasts that meet me run away for fear.
Therefore no marvel though Demetrius   100
Do, as[80] a monster, fly my presence thus.
What wicked[81] and dissembling glass[82] of mine
Made me compare[83] with Hermia's sphery[84] eyne?[85]
But who is here? Lysander, on the ground?
Dead, or asleep? I see no blood, no wound   105
Lysander, if you live, good sir, awake.
Lysander (*waking*) And run through fire I will for thy sweet sake,
Transparent[86] Helena! Nature shows[87] art,[88]
That through thy bosom makes me see thy heart.
Where is Demetrius? O, how fit a word[89]   110

76 my prayer = I entreat/supplicate/appeal
77 reward
78 adorable
79 drawing toward oneself as if by magnetic powers
80 as if I were
81 hateful, disastrous, perverted, malicious
82 dissembling glass = deceiving/hypocritical mirror
83 be compared to, set in rivalry with★
84 like the heavenly spheres
85 made ME comPARE with HERMya's SPHERy EYNE
86 diaphanous (that is, penetrated by light)
87 (verb) displays, exhibits
88 skill, workmanship, artifice (as opposed to Nature's usual inherent/invariable
    procedures)
89 where IS deMETRus O how FIT a WORD

Is that vile name to perish on my sword!

Helena   Do not say so, Lysander, say not so.

What though he love your Hermia? Lord, what though?[90]

Yet Hermia still loves you. Then be content.

115 *Lysander* Content with Hermia? No. I do repent

The tedious[91] minutes I with her have spent.

Not Hermia but Helena I love.

Who will not change a raven[92] for a dove?[93]

The will of man is by his reason swayed,[94]

120 And reason says you are the worthier maid.

Things growing are not ripe, until their season.[95]

So I, being young, till now ripe not to[96] reason.

And touching[97] now[98] the point[99] of human skill,

Reason becomes[100] the marshal to[101] my will,

125 And leads me to your eyes, where I o'erlook[102]

Love's stories[103] written in love's richest book.[104]

---

90 what though? = what difference does it make that he does?

91 wearisome, long, vexatious

92 a bird that is black

93 a bird that in its noblest form is white as snow

94 moved, bent, influenced

95 time

96 ripe not to = not yet ready for

97 reaching, attaining

98 as opposed to when he was young

99 height, highest part

100 thus becomes

101 marshal to = officer in charge of

102 perceive, read through, examine

103 histories, true accounts

104 richest book = most exalted/abundant/valuable source of instruction (that is, her eyes, which are the road to her heart)

Helena   Wherefore[105] was I to this keen[106] mockery born?
    When at your hands did I deserve this scorn?
    Is't not enough, is't not enough, young man,
    That I did never, no, nor never can   130
    Deserve a sweet look from Demetrius' eye,
    But you must flout[107] my insufficiency?[108]
    Good troth, you do me wrong, good sooth, you do,
    In such disdainful manner me to woo.
    But fare you well. Perforce I must confess   135
    I thought you lord[109] of more true gentleness.
    O that a lady, of[110] one man refused,
    Should of another therefore be abused![111]

EXIT

Lysander   She sees not[112] Hermia. Hermia, sleep thou there,
    And never mayst thou come Lysander near!   140
    For as a surfeit of the sweetest things
    The deepest loathing to the stomach brings,
    Or as the heresies that men do leave[113]
    Are hated most of[114] those they did deceive,
    So thou, my surfeit and my heresy,   145

105 for what purpose, why* (accented on either syllable, it is here pronounced
    whereFORE)
106 harsh, cruel
107 scoff, jeer at, mock
108 INsufFISHenSIGH
109 master, possessor
110 by
111 wronged, imposed on
112 sees not = does not see (has not seen)
113 abandon, quit, forsake
114 by

Of[115] all be hated, but the most of me.
And, all my powers,[116] address[117] your love and might
To honor Helen and to be her knight.

EXIT

Hermia (*awaking*) Help me, Lysander, help me! Do thy best
150   To pluck[118] this crawling serpent from my breast!
Ay me, for pity.[119] What a dream was here.
Lysander, look how I do quake[120] with fear.
Methought a serpent eat[121] my heart away,
And you sat smiling at his cruel prey.[122]
155   Lysander? What, removed?[123] Lysander? Lord,[124]
What, out of hearing? Gone? No sound, no word?
Alack,[125] where are you? Speak, an if[126] you hear.
Speak, of all loves![127] I swoon almost[128] with fear.
No? Then I well perceive you are not nigh.
160   Either death or you I'll find immediately.[129]

EXIT

TITANIA SLEEPS ON

115 by
116 qualities, capacities ("faculties")
117 raise up, prepare, make ready
118 pull off
119 for pity = for goodness sake
120 tremble, shake
121 ate (ET)
122 violence, pillage
123 retired
124 good Lord
125 exclamation of surprise and distress
126 an if = if
127 of all loves = by/in the name of all true love (?)
128 swoon almost = almost swoon
129 either DEATH or YOU i'll FIND imMEEDyetLIE

Act 3

SCENE I

The wood, Titania lying asleep

ENTER QUINCE, SNUG, BOTTOM, FLUTE,
SNOUT, AND STARVELING

Bottom Are we all met?[1]

Quince Pat,[2] pat. And here's a marvelous[3] convenient place for
  our rehearsal. This green plot shall be our stage, this
  hawthorn brake[4] our tiring house,[5] and we will do it in
  action, as we will do it before the Duke.   5

Bottom Peter Quince?

Quince What sayest thou,[6] bully[7] Bottom?

Bottom There are things in this comedy of Pyramus and Thisbe

---

1 Are we all met = have we all come, are we all here
2 promptly, on time, exactly★
3 (adverb)
4 hawthorn brake = thicket/clump of small, flowering shrubs★
5 tiring house = dressing room
6 sayest thou = have you got to say
7 worthy, admirable

that will never please. First, Pyramus must draw a sword to kill
10   himself, which the ladies cannot abide. How answer you that?

Snout   By'r lakin,[8] a parlous[9] fear.

Starveling I believe we must leave the killing out, when all is
done.

Bottom   Not a whit.[10] I have a device[11] to make all well.
15   Write me a prologue, and let the prologue seem to[12] say we
will do no harm with our swords, and that Pyramus is not
killed indeed.[13] And for the more better assurance, tell them
that I, Pyramus, am not Pyramus, but Bottom the weaver.
This will put them out[14] of fear.

20 *Quince*   Well, we will have such a prologue, and it shall be
written in eight and six.[15]

Bottom   No, make it two more. Let it be written in eight and
eight.[16]

Snout   Will not the ladies be afeard of the lion?

25 *Starveling* I fear it, I promise you.

Bottom   Masters, you ought to consider with[17] yourselves to[18]
bring in − God shield[19] us! − a lion among ladies, is a most

---

  8 by'r lakin = by our little Lady (the Virgin Mary)
  9 risky, awkward, dangerous
10 bit (the least / smallest particle)
11 plan, way, invention
12 seem to = (1) vouchsafe, confirm, (2) properly / fittingly
13 really, in fact / truth ("in deed")
14 put them out = cause them to be / make them free of
15 ballad meter: lines of 8 syllables (4 metric feet) followed by lines of 6 syllables
    (3 metric feet)
16 iambic tetrameter
17 for
18 that to
19 protect

dreadful thing. For there is not a more fearful wildfowl[20] than your lion living.[21] And we ought to look to 't.[22]

Snout   Therefore another prologue must tell he is not a lion.   30

Bottom   Nay. You must name his name, and half his face must be seen through the lion's neck, and he himself must speak through, saying thus, or to the same defect[23] – "Ladies" – or "Fair ladies, I would wish you" – or "I would request you" – or "I would entreat you not to fear, not to tremble. My life for   35 yours. If you think I come hither as a lion, it were pity of my life.[24] No, I am no such thing, I am a man as other men are." And there indeed let him name his name, and tell them plainly he is Snug the joiner.

Quince   Well. It shall be so. But there is[25] two hard things: that is,   40 to bring the moonlight into a chamber,[26] for you know Pyramus and Thisbe meet by moonlight.

Snout   Doth the moon shine that night we play our play?

Bottom   A calendar, a calendar![27] Look in the almanac. Find out moonshine, find out moonshine.   45

Quince   Yes, it doth shine that night.

Bottom   Why, then may you leave a casement[28] of the great chamber window, where we play, open, and the moon may shine in at the casement.

Quince   Ay. Or else one must come in with a bush of thorns and   50

20 (as he has done before, and will do again, Bottom mangles the language)
21 (1) when it is still living, (2) anywhere among living creatures
22 look to't = beware, be careful
23 effect (not defect) = purpose, significance
24 it were pity of my life = it would be regrettable/shameful for my life/me
25 (there is: Elizabethan grammatical usage was flexible)
26 room
27 (calendars often listed astronomical data, thus calendar = almanac)
28 window frame/sash (sometimes hinged)

a lanthorn,[29] and say he comes to disfigure,[30] or to present,[31] the person of Moonshine. Then there is another thing. We must have a wall in the great chamber. For Pyramus and Thisbe, says the story, did talk through the chink[32] of a wall.

55   *Snout*   You can never bring in a wall. What say you, Bottom?

     Bottom   Some man or other must present Wall. And let him have some plaster, or some loam,[33] or some rough-cast[34] about him, to signify wall, or let him hold his fingers thus. And through that cranny shall Pyramus and Thisbe whisper.

60   *Quince*   If that may be, then all is well. Come, sit down, every mother's son, and rehearse your parts. Pyramus, you begin. When you have spoken your speech, enter[35] into that brake, and so every one according to his cue.

ENTER Puck BEHIND

     Puck   What hempen homespuns[36] have we swaggering[37]
65   here,
     So near the cradle[38] of the Fairy Queen?
     What, a play toward?[39] I'll be an auditor — [40]
     An actor too, perhaps, if I see cause.

---

29 lantern* (a description drawn from that of the Man in the Moon, seen as he gathered firewood)
30 figure = represent, portray; disfigure = deform, destroy
31 (verb) represent*
32 fissure, crack*
33 clay, mud
34 mixture of lime and gravel
35 go
36 hempen homespuns = rustics (wearing garments made of coarse homespun hemp)
37 behaving insolently, acting superior
38 sleeping place, bed
39 approaching, about to be, coming
40 WHAT a PLAY toWARD i'll BE an AUDitor (?)

Quince Speak, Pyramus. Thisbe, stand forth.

Bottom Thisbe, the flowers of odious[41] savors[42] sweet –   70

Quince (*correcting him*) Odorous,[43] odorous.

Bottom   – odorous savors

sweet.

So hath thy breath, my dearest Thisbe dear.

But hark, a voice! Stay thou but here awhile,

And by and by[44] I will to thee appear.

EXIT BOTTOM

Puck A stranger Pyramus than e'er played,[45] here.   75

EXIT PUCK

Flute Must[46] I speak now?

Quince Ay, marry, must you. For you must understand he[47] goes
but[48] to see a noise that he heard, and is to come again.

Flute Most radiant Pyramus, most lily white of hue,

Of color like the red rose on triumphant[49] brier,   80

Most brisky juvenal[50] and eke[51] most lovely Jew,[52]

As true as truest horse that yet would never tire,[53]

---

41 odious = repulsive, offensive
42 scent, perfume
43 sweet smelling, fragrant
44 by and by = immediately, at once
45 e'er played = was ever* acted/performed/staged
46 should*
47 Bottom, playing Pyramus
48 only
49 conquering (that is, the rose has succeeded in growing on/over the brier)
50 brisky juvenal = actively/sprightly juvenile/youth
51 also (archaic even in Shakespeare's time: used satirically)
52 (used [1] for the rhyme and [2] satirically: Jews being regarded negatively, the
   word *lovely* makes no great sense)
53 (again, used for the rhyme: being a faithful horse has little or nothing to do
   with endurance)

I'll meet thee, Pyramus, at Ninny's[54] tomb.

Quince (*correcting him*) "Ninus' tomb," man. Why, you must not

85   speak that yet. That you answer[55] to Pyramus. You speak[56] all
          your part at once, cues and all.

          (*calling*) Pyramus, enter! Your cue is past — it is "never tire."

Flute   O, as true as truest horse, that yet would never tire.

ENTER PUCK, AND BOTTOM, NOW WITH AN ASS'S HEAD

Bottom If I were fair, Thisbe, I were only thine.[57]

90   *Quince* O monstrous! O strange! We are haunted.[58] Pray
          masters! Fly masters! Help!

EXEUNT QUINCE, SNUG, FLUTE, SNOUT, AND STARVELING

Puck   I'll follow you,[59] I'll lead you about a round,
              Through bog, through bush, through brake, through brier.
              Sometime a horse I'll be, sometime a hound,

95   A hog, a headless bear, sometime a fire,
              And neigh, and bark, and grunt, and roar, and burn,
              Like horse, hound, hog, bear, fire, at every turn.[60]

EXIT PUCK

Bottom Why do they run away? This is a knavery[61] of them, to
          make me afeard.

54 (satirical: ninny = simpleton, fool; Ninus = husband of Semiramis and
   founder of Nineveh)
55 should say in answer to
56 are speaking
57 (Bottom's language-mangling: if I were fair = if it is true that I am
   handsome; I were only thine = I would still be only yours)
58 beset by spirits/specters/imaginary beings★
59 the five fleeing men
60 like HORSE hound HOG bear FIRE at EVry TURN (this particular
   scansion is strictly by convention: see Raffel, *From Stress to Stress,* xvii–xviii)
61 trickery, roguery★

ENTER SNOUT

Snout   O Bottom, thou art changed. What do I see on thee?   100
Bottom   What do you see? You see an asshead of your own.
   Do you?

EXIT SNOUT

ENTER QUINCE

Quince   Bless thee, Bottom, bless thee! Thou art translated.[62]

EXIT QUINCE

Bottom   I see their knavery. This is to make an ass of me, to fright
   me, if they could. But I will not stir from this place, do what   105
   they can. I will walk up and down here, and I will sing, that[63]
   they shall hear I am not afraid.

SINGS

   The ousel[64] cock so black of hue,
      With orange[65] tawny bill,
   The throstle[66] with his note[67] so true,   110
      The wren with little quill[68] –
Titania   (*waking*) What angel wakes me from my flow'ry bed?
Bottom   (*singing*)
   The finch, the sparrow and the lark,
      The plainsong[69] cuckoo gray,   115

62 transformed*
63 so that
64 blackbird
65 orangelike (bisyllabic)
66 thrush
67 song
68 voice/song? feathers, plumage?
69 producing simple melodies

Whose note full many a man doth mark,[70]
    And dares not answer nay —
for, indeed, who would set his wit to[71] so foolish a bird?
Who would give a bird the lie, though he cry "cuckoo"[72]
120   never so?[73]

Titania I pray thee, gentle mortal, sing again.
Mine ear is much enamored of thy note.
So is mine eye enthrallèd to thy shape,
And thy fair virtue's force[74] perforce doth move me
125   On the first view to say, to swear,[75] I love thee.

Bottom Methinks, mistress,[76] you should have little reason for
that. And yet, to say the truth, reason and love keep little
company together nowadays. The more the pity, that some
honest[77] neighbors will not make them[78] friends. Nay, I can
130   gleek[79] upon occasion.

Titania Thou art as wise as thou art beautiful.

Bottom Not so, neither. But if I had[80] wit enough to get out of
this wood, I have enough to serve mine own turn.[81]

Titania Out of this wood do not desire to go.
135   Thou shalt[82] remain here, whether thou wilt or no.

---

70 notice, observe★
71 wit to = mental capacity★ against
72 cuckold
73 so much/often
74 vigor, strength, energy
75 (to swear — and most solemnly — meant a great deal more than it does today)
76 (a form of address, more like Ma'am or Madam★)
77 respectable, honorable★
78 (that is, truth, reason, and love)
79 play word games
80 if I had = granted that/even though/as sure as I have
81 devices, stratagems
82 must

I am a spirit of no common rate.[83]
The summer, still,[84] doth tend[85] upon my state,[86]
And I do love thee. Therefore, go with me.
I'll give thee fairies to attend on thee.
And they shall fetch thee jewels from the deep,   140
And sing while thou on pressèd flowers dost sleep.
And I will purge[87] thy mortal grossness[88] so,
That thou shalt like an airy[89] spirit go.[90]
Peaseblossom![91] Cobweb! Moth! and Mustardseed!

ENTER PEASEBLOSSOM, COBWEB, MOTH,
AND MUSTARDSEED

Peaseblossom Ready.
Cobweb   And I.
Moth   And I.
Mustardseed   And I.
All   Where shall[92] we go?   145
Titania   Be kind[93] and courteous to this gentleman,
Hop in[94] his walks and gambol in his eyes,[95]
Feed him with apricocks and dewberries,[96]

83 standing, rank
84 always, forever
85 attends, follows
86 condition, state of health/welfare
87 cleanse, purify
88 density, solidity, materiality
89 ethereal
90 live and move
91 the flowers of peas and other related vegetables
92 must
93 proper
94 during, on
95 gambol in his eyes = dance/spring in his sight/where he can see you
96 apricocks and dewberries = apricots and blackberries/gooseberries

With purple grapes, green figs, and mulberries,
150   The honey bags steal from the humble bees,[97]
  And for night-tapers[98] crop[99] their waxen thighs
  And light them at[100] the fiery glow worm's eyes,
  To have[101] my love to bed and to arise,
  And pluck the wings from painted[102] butterflies
155   To fan the moonbeams from his sleeping eyes.
  Nod[103] to him, elves, and do him courtesies.[104]

Peaseblossom Hail, mortal!

Cobweb   Hail!

Moth   Hail!

Mustardseed   Hail!

Bottom   I cry your worships mercy,[105] heartily.[106]
  (*to Cobweb*) I beseech your worship's name?[107]

160 *Cobweb*   Cobweb.

Bottom   I shall desire you of more acquaintance,[108] good
  Master Cobweb. If I cut my finger, I shall make bold[109] with
  you. (*to Peaseblossom*) Your name, honest gentleman?

Peaseblossom Peaseblossom.

---

97 steal the honey bags (storage sacs for honey) from the humble bees
98 nighttime candles
99 cut/lop off
100 by contact with
101 lead, convey
102 brightly colored
103 (as a salutation)
104 CORteSIZE
105 cry your worships mercy = beg your pardon, distinguished/honorable personages
106 with genuine sincerity/cordiality
107 entreat/implore/earnestly request
108 desire you of more acquaintance = want better/further acquaintance with you
109 make bold = take liberties, presume (cobwebs have long been — and still are — used to staunch bleeding)

Bottom   I pray you, commend me[110] to Mistress Squash,   165
your mother, and to Master Peascod,[111] your father. Good
Master Peaseblossom, I shall desire you of more acquaintance,
too. (*to Mustardseed*) Your name, I beseech you, sir?

Mustardseed   Mustardseed.

Bottom   Good Master Mustardseed, I know your   170
patience[112] well. That same[113] cowardly[114] giant-like
ox-beef[115] hath devoured[116] many a gentleman of your
house.[117] I promise you your kindred had[118] made my eyes
water, ere now. I desire your more acquaintance, good Master
Mustardseed.   175

Titania   Come, wait upon him. Lead him to my bower.
The moon, methinks, looks with a wat'ry eye,
And when she weeps, weeps every little flower,[119]
Lamenting some enforcèd chastity.[120]
Tie up my lover's tongue,[121] bring him silently.[122]   180

EXEUNT

110 commend me = convey my greetings to (conventionally – and here
     comically – polite)
111 pea pod
112 calm composure, forbearance (a comic reference to mustard's proverbial
     pungency)
113 very
114 cowardly giant-like: cowardly because a mustard seed is so much the smaller
     of the two
115 ox meat
116 devoured: beef being eaten with mustard
117 family, lineage
118 have
119 and when the Moon weeps, every little flower weeps also (the Moon was
     considered the source of dew; she was also the goddess of chastity)
120 enforcèd chastity = violated virginity, forced rape (CHAStiTIE)
121 (Titania has been made foolish by Oberon's magic, but she has managed to
     notice how fond Bottom is of the sound of his own voice)
122 tie UP my LOver's TONGUE bring him SIlentLIE

SCENE 2

Another part of the wood

ENTER OBERON

Oberon I wonder if Titania be awaked,
  Then what it was that next[1] came in her eye,
  Which she must dote on in extremity.[2]

ENTER PUCK

  Here comes my messenger. How now, mad[3] spirit?
5 What night-rule[4] now about this haunted grove?
Puck   My mistress with a monster is in love,
  Near to her close and consecrated bower.[5]
  While she was in her dull[6] and sleeping hour,
  A crew of patches,[7] rude mechanicals,[8]
10 That work for bread[9] upon Athenian stalls,[10]
  Were met together to rehearse a play
  Intended for great Theseus' nuptial-day.
  The shallowest thick-skin[11] of that barren sort,[12]
  Who Pyramus presented in their sport,

1 immediately following
2 in extremity = with inordinate/extraordinary intensity (exTREmiTIE)
3 wild
4 nighttime conduct/behavior
5 close and consecrated bower = secluded/secret/private and sanctified/
  hallowed boudoir/bedroom
6 inactive, sluggish
7 clowns, fools
8 rude mechanicals = uneducated/ignorant artisans★
9 for bread = for their livelihood
10 upon Athenian stalls = in the shops/stores of Athens
11 shallowest thick-skin = most superficial unrefined/obtuse fellow
12 barren sort = meager/arid/dull rank/kind

Forsook his scene[13] and entered in a brake,   15
When I did him at this advantage take.[14]
An ass's nole[15] I fixèd[16] on his head.
Anon his Thisbe must be answerèd,
And forth my mimic[17] comes. When they him spy,[18]
As[19] wild geese that the creeping fowler[20] eye,   20
Or russet-pated choughs,[21] many in sort,[22]
Rising and cawing at the gun's report,
Sever[23] themselves and madly sweep[24] the sky.
So, at his[25] sight, away his fellows fly,
And, at our[26] stamp, here o'er and o'er one[27] falls.   25
He murder cries,[28] and help from Athens calls.
Their sense[29] thus weak, lost with their fears thus[30] strong,
Made senseless[31] things begin to do them wrong,
For briers and thorns at their apparel snatch.

13 forsook his scene = broke off/left his stage-performance/play
14 at this advantage take = in this favorable time/occasion/opportunity catch/
   lay hold of ★
15 noddle, pate ("top of the head")
16 fastened, attached
17 buffoon, droll/grotesque actor
18 see, behold
19 like
20 bird hunter
21 russet-pated choughs = reddish brown–headed crows (CHUFFS)
22 many in sort = a large flock
23 disunite, scatter
24 pass swiftly across
25 Bottom's
26 my (Puck's)
27 one of them
28 murder cries = cries murder
29 perceptive faculties
30 in this degree/manner
31 inanimate

30   Some sleeves, some hats, from yielders[32] all things catch.
        I led them on in this distracted[33] fear,
        And left sweet Pyramus translated there.
        When in that moment, so it came to pass,
        Titania waked, and straightway loved an ass.
35 *Oberon* This falls out[34] better than I could devise.[35]
        But hast thou yet latched[36] the Athenian's eyes
        With the love juice, as I did bid thee do?
    Puck I took him sleeping – that is finished, too –
        And the Athenian woman by his side,
40   That, when he waked, of force[37] she must be eyed.[38]

                ENTER HERMIA AND DEMETRIUS

    Oberon   Stand close: this is the same Athenian.[39]
    Puck   This is the woman, but not this the man.
    Demetrius O why rebuke[40] you him that loves you so?
        Lay breath so bitter[41] on your bitter foe.
45 *Hermia*   Now I but chide.[42] But I should use[43] thee worse,
        For thou, I fear, hast given me cause to curse.[44]
        If thou hast slain Lysander in his sleep,

32 he who thus surrenders
33 confused, perplexed
34 falls out = happens, comes to pass, proves
35 plan, invent, contrive
36 wet, moistened
37 necessity
38 seen
39 athEENiyAN
40 (1) reprove/chide/blame/shame severely, (2) repress, check, despise
41 unpleasant, grievous
42 but chide = only loudly express dissatisfaction/scold★
43 should use = ought to speak to/treat
44 invoke the wrath of God/divine vengeance

Being o'er shoes[45] in blood, plunge in the deep[46]
And kill me too.
The sun was not so true unto the day   50
As he to me. Would he have stolen away
From sleeping Hermia? I'll believe as soon
This whole[47] earth may be bored[48] and that the moon
May through the center creep, and so displease[49]
Her brother's[50] noontide with th'Antipodes.[51]   55
It cannot be but[52] thou hast murdered him:
So should a murderer look, so dead,[53] so grim.[54]

Demetrius So should the murdered look, and so should I,
Pierced through the heart with your stern cruelty.[55]
Yet you, the murderer,[56] look as bright, as clear,   60
As yonder Venus in her glimmering sphere.

Hermia   What's this to[57] my Lysander? Where is he?
Ah, good Demetrius, wilt thou give him me?

Demetrius I had rather give his carcass to my hounds.

45 shoe deep (it is the "v" which has been elided, so "o'er" remains bisyllabic:
    Oer)
46 in the deep = to the depths
47 (1) entire, (2) unbroken, intact
48 pierced, run through
49 displease . . . with = offend / vex by bringing in night / darkness (it is the
    Sun's noontide which is displeased, not the Sun himself)
50 brother = fellow creature, one of the same employment / profession,
    comrade (a reference to the Sun)
51 people who live on exactly opposite sides of the earth (anTIpoDEEZ)
52 cannot be but = can only be that
53 benumbed, pale, lifeless
54 cruel, harsh
55 CRUelTIE
56 (possibly bisyllabic – or close to bisyllabic)
57 what's this to = what has this to do with

65 *Hermia*   Out dog, out cur! Thou driv'st me past the bounds[58]
        Of maiden's patience. Hast thou slain him, then?
        Henceforth be never numbered[59] among men.
        O, once[60] tell true. Tell true, even[61] for my sake!
        Durst thou have looked upon him, being[62] awake?
70   And hast thou killed him sleeping? O brave touch![63]
        Could not a worm,[64] an adder, do so[65] much?
        An adder did[66] it. For with doubler tongue
        Than thine, thou serpent, never adder stung.
    Demetrius You spend[67] your passion on a misprised mood.[68]
75   I am not guilty of Lysander's blood.
        Nor is he dead, for aught[69] that I can tell.
    Hermia   I pray thee, tell me then that he is well.
    Demetrius An if I could, what should I get therefore?[70]
    Hermia   A privilege[71] never to see me more.[72]
80   And from thy hated presence part I so.
        See me no more, whether he be dead or no.[73]

EXIT HERMIA

58 limits
59 counted
60 (1) just, (2) once and for all
61 just
62 you (Demetrius) being
63 brave touch = daring/courageous/splendid/fine act/deed/blow/stroke
64 snake, reptile
65 as
66 did do
67 (1) expend, employ, (2) exhaust, waste, wear out
68 misprised mood = mistaken★ thought/feeling
69 anything
70 for that
71 right, permission, license
72 aPRIviLEDGE NEver to SEE me MORE
73 see ME no MORE whether HE be DEAD or NO

Demetrius   There is no following[74] her in this fierce vein.[75]
 Here therefore for a while I will remain.
 So sorrow's heaviness[76] doth heavier grow.
 For debt[77] that bankrupt[78] sleep doth sorrow owe,   85
 Which now in some slight measure[79] it[80] will pay,
 If for his tender[81] here I make some stay.[82]

DEMETRIUS LIES DOWN AND SLEEPS

Oberon   What hast thou done? Thou hast mistaken quite,
 And laid the love juice on some true love's sight.
 Of thy misprision must perforce ensue[83]   90
 Some true love turned,[84] and not a false turned true.
Puck   Then fate o'errules,[85] that[86] one man holding[87] troth,
 A million fail,[88] confounding[89] oath on oath.
Oberon   About the wood go[90] swifter than the wind,[91]

74 pursuing, chasing after
75 mood, disposition, humor
76 burden, oppression, displeasure, melancholy
77 the debt
78 exhausted
79 quantity, degree, duration
80 sleep
81 his tender = sleep's offer* of payment to sorrow (to forestall a bankruptcy lawsuit)
82 stop, pause (noun)
83 follow (of THY misPREEzhun MUST perFORCE enSYUE)
84 reversed
85 prevails, governs
86 so that for
87 keeping
88 are deficient/lacking, fall short, break down, disappoint
89 destroying, breaking
90 you must go
91 (rhymes with find, kind, bind, etc.)

95   And Helena of Athens look thou find.

        All fancy-sick[92] she is, and pale of cheer,[93]

        With sighs[94] of love that costs the fresh blood dear.[95]

        By some illusion[96] see thou[97] bring her here.

        I'll charm his eyes against[98] she do appear.

100 *Puck*   I go, I go, look how I go,

        Swifter than arrow from the Tartar's bow.[99]

EXIT PUCK

OBERON, CHANTING, PUTS LOVE JUICE IN DEMETRIUS' EYES

Oberon   Flower of this purple dye,[100]

        Hit with Cupid's archery,

        Sink in apple[101] of his eye.

105   When his love he doth espy,

        Let her shine as gloriously[102]

        As the Venus of the sky.

        When thou wak'st, if she be by,

        Beg of her for remedy.[103]

ENTER PUCK

92 lovesick
93 face, countenance
94 (sighs, for love or any other reason, were long thought to produce negative physical consequences)
95 a high price★ (adverb)
96 deception, delusion
97 see thou = make sure that you
98 in preparation for when
99 (Tartar bows were stronger)
100 (magical incantations often have, as here, only a single rhyme: A A A A A A A A)
101 pupil
102 GLORyusLIE
103 cure

Puck   Captain[104] of our fairy band,   110

      Helena is here at hand,

      And the youth, mistook by me,

      Pleading for a lover's fee.[105]

      Shall we their fond pageant[106] see?

      Lord, what fools these mortals be!   115

Oberon   Stand aside.[107] The noise they make

      Will cause Demetrius to awake.

Puck   Then will two at once woo one:

      That must needs be sport alone.[108]

      And those things do best please me   120

      That befall prepost'rously.[109]

ENTER LYSANDER AND HELENA

Lysander   Why should you think that I should[110] woo in
      scorn?

      Scorn and derision[111] never come in[112] tears.

      Look when I vow,[113] I weep. And vows so born

      In their nativity[114] all truth appears.   125

      How can these things in me seem scorn to you,

---

104 head, chief
105 payment, reward
106 scene, drama
107 to the far side of the stage (where actors could be seen/heard by the
    audience, but not by actors elsewhere on the stage)
108 having no equal
109 nonsensically, irrationally, perversely, monstrously
110 would, would wish to
111 mockery, ridicule*
112 with, together with
113 solemnly promise/declare
114 birth

Bearing the badge[115] of faith to prove them true?

Helena   You do advance[116] your cunning, more and more,
            When truth kills truth, O devilish holy fray![117]
130   These vows are Hermia's.[118] Will you give her o'er?[119]
            Weigh oath with[120] oath, and you will nothing weigh.
            Your vows to her and me, put in two scales,[121]
            Will even[122] weigh, and both as light as tales.[123]

Lysander   I had no judgment,[124] when to her I swore.

135 Helena Nor none, in my mind, now you give her o'er.

Lysander   Demetrius loves her, and he loves not you.

Demetrius (waking) O Helena, goddess, nymph, perfect,[125]
            divine,
            To what, my love, shall I compare thine eyne!
            Crystal is muddy.[126] O how ripe in show[127]
140   Thy lips, those kissing cherries, tempting grow!
            That[128] pure congealèd[129] white, high Taurus snow,[130]

---

115 mark, emblem
116 accelerate, improve
117 combat, fighting★
118 are Hermia's = belong to Hermia
119 give her o'er = surrender/give up/abandon her
120 together with/against
121 pans (scales commonly balanced a known weight in one pan against an
    unknown weight in the other pan)
122 evenly, the same
123 idle stories, lies
124 faculty of judging, discernment ("maturity")
125 (having begun as "parfit," the word may very well be pronounced, here,
    perFECT
126 unclear, turgid, dull
127 ripe in show = like ripe fruit ("red and full") in appearance
128 so that
129 frozen
130 Taurus snow = snow on Mt. Taurus (in southern Turkey)

Fanned with the eastern wind, turns to a crow
When thou hold'st up thy hand. O let me kiss
This princess of pure white, this seal[131] of bliss.

Helena O spite! O hell![132] I see you all are bent[133]   145
To set against[134] me for your merriment.
If you[135] were civil, and knew courtesy,
You would not do me thus much injury.
Can you not[136] hate me, as I know you do,
But you must[137] join in souls[138] to mock me too?   150
If you[139] were men, as men you are in show,
You would not use a gentle lady so,
To vow, and swear, and superpraise[140] my parts,[141]
When I am sure you hate me with your hearts.
You both are rivals, and love Hermia.   155
And now both rivals, to mock[142] Helena.
A trim exploit,[143] a manly enterprise,
To conjure tears up,[144] in a poor maid's eyes,
With your derision. None of noble sort

131 pledge (a woman giving her hand = promising to marry)
132 (not a curse/imprecation, but an invocation of the infernal nature/origin
    of the torments being inflicted on her)
133 determined
134 set against = be hostile to/attack
135 Demetrius
136 can you not = can't you (is it not possible for you)
137 but you must = without your having to
138 join in souls = join in fellowship/together
139 Demetrius and Lysander
140 overpraise
141 qualities, abilities, talents, character
142 to mock = in mocking
143 trim exploit = fine/excellent/proper enterprise/deed
144 conjure . . . up = magically produce

160   Would so offend a virgin, and extort[145]

       A poor soul's patience, all to make you sport.

    Lysander   You are unkind, Demetrius. Be not so.

       For you love Hermia: this you know I know.[146]

       And here, with all good will, with all my heart,

165   In Hermia's love I yield you up my part.[147]

       And yours of Helena to me bequeath,[148]

       Whom I do love, and will do till my death.[149]

    Helena   Never did mockers waste more idle[150] breath.

    Demetrius Lysander, keep thy Hermia. I will none.[151]

170   If e'er I loved her, all that love is gone.

       My heart to her but as guest-wise sojourned,[152]

       And now to Helen is it home returned,

       There to remain.

    Lysander   Helen, it is not so.

    Demetrius Disparage[153] not the faith thou dost not know,

175   Lest, to thy peril, thou aby[154] it dear.[155]

       Look where thy love comes; yonder is thy dear.[156]

145 intimidate, torture, abuse (verb)
146 for YOU love HERmia THIS you KNOW i KNOW
147 share
148 transfer, give (and YOURS of HEleNA to ME beQUEATH – but see note
    150)
149 (death and bequeath are either an eye-rhyme – that is, spelling rhymes, but
    not sound – or more probably, since this is a triple rhyme, and breath =
    breth, bequeath is pronounced beeQUETH)
150 useless, vacant, frivolous
151 will none = want none of her ("do not want her")
152 but as guest-wise sojourned = visited/lodged, temporarily, only as a guest
    (my HEART to HER but AS guestWISE soJOURNED)
153 discredit, degrade, dishonor
154 redeem, pay/atone for, purchase★
155 (adverb)
156 (identical rhyme was not frowned upon; further, these identically spelled

ENTER HERMIA

Hermia   Dark night, that from the eye his function[157] takes,

The ear more quick of apprehension[158] makes.

Wherein[159] it doth impair[160] the seeing sense,

It pays[161] the hearing double recompense.[162]   180

Thou art not by mine eye, Lysander, found:

Mine ear, I thank it, brought me to thy sound.

But why unkindly[163] didst thou leave me so?

Lysander   Why should he[164] stay, whom love doth press[165] to go?

Hermia   What love could press Lysander from my side?   185

Lysander   Lysander's love, that would not let him bide:[166]

Fair Helena, who more engilds[167] the night

Than all yon fiery oes[168] and eyes[169] of light.

Why seek'st thou me? Could not this make thee know

The hate I bear thee made me leave thee so?   190

Hermia   You speak not as you think. It cannot be.

Helena   Lo, she is one of this confederacy.[170]

---

and sounded words are syntactically different, one an adverb, the other a
noun)

157 his function = its operation

158 perception

159 when ("in the respect in which")

160 weaken

161 gives, rewards, returns

162 compensation, satisfaction, restitution

163 (1) improperly, unnaturally, (2) unpleasantly

164 anyone

165 force, drive

166 remain

167 brightens with gold light

168 orbs ("spangles")

169 stars

170 conspiracy, compact, league

Now I perceive they have conjoined[171] all three
To fashion[172] this false[173] sport, in spite of me.
195 Injurious[174] Hermia, most ungrateful maid,[175]
Have you conspired, have you with these contrived[176]
To bait[177] me with this foul derision?
Is all the counsel that we two have shared,
The sisters' vows, the hours that we have spent
200 When we have chid the hasty-footed[178] time
For parting us – O, is all forgot?[179]
All school days' friendship, childhood innocence?
We, Hermia, like two artificial[180] gods,
Have with our needles[181] created both[182] one flower,
205 Both on one sampler,[183] sitting on one cushion,
Both warbling of one song, both in one key,
As if our hands, our sides, voices and minds,
Had been incorporate.[184] So we grew together,[185]

171 combined, united
172 shape, form (verb)
173 lying, treacherous, deceitful
174 offensive, insulting
175 inDJURyus HERmia MOST unGRATEful MAID (more weakly
     accented syllables, like the last two in Hermia, are amenable to metrical
     ellision: HERMya)
176 plotted, planned, concocted
177 harass, persecute, torment
178 hasty footed = swiftly walking
179 for PARTing US O is ALL forGOT (syntactic pause, like that after "us," can
     act as a metrical pause)
180 (1) make believe, fictitious, (2) artful, skillful
181 sewing needles
182 together
183 (1) embroidered canvas, (2) model, pattern
184 united
185 had BEEN inCORPrate SO we GREW toGETHer

Like to a double cherry, seeming parted,
But yet an union in partition,[186]   210
Two lovely berries moulded[187] on one stem:
So[188] with two seeming[189] bodies, but one heart,
Two of the first,[190] like coats[191] in heraldry,
Due[192] but to one and crownèd with one crest.[193]
And will you rent[194] our ancient[195] love asunder,[196]   215
To join with men in scorning your poor friend?
It is not friendly, 'tis not maidenly.
Our sex, as well as I, may chide you for it,
Though I alone do feel the injury.

Hermia I am amazèd[197] at your passionate[198] words.   220
I scorn you not. It seems that you scorn me.

Helena Have you not set Lysander, as in scorn,
To follow me and praise my eyes and face?
And made your other love, Demetrius,
Who even but now did spurn[199] me with his foot,   225
To call me goddess, nymph, divine and rare,
Precious, celestial? Wherefore speaks he this

186 parTIsiON
187 shaped, formed (as if in a mold)
188 thus
189 apparent
190 (the first color noted in technical heraldic descriptions)
191 coats of arms
192 belonging/owing to
193 (figure/device on a wreath, once worn on a knight's helmet, and in
   heraldic coat of arms set above both helmet and shield)
194 tear, pull asunder ("rend")
195 bygone, former
196 apart
197 bewildered, perplexed, astonished
198 hot-tempered, angry, vehement
199 kick, thrust

To her he hates? And wherefore doth Lysander
Deny your love, so rich within his soul,
230   And tender me, forsooth,[200] affection,[201]
But[202] by your setting on,[203] by your consent?
What though I be not so in grace as you,[204]
So hung upon[205] with love, so fortunate?[206]
(But miserable[207] most, to love unloved)
235   This you should pity rather than despise.
     Hermia   I understand not what you mean by this.
     Helena   Ay, do, persever,[208] counterfeit[209] sad[210] looks,
Make mouths[211] upon me when I turn my back,
Wink each at other, hold the sweet jest up.[212]
240   This sport, well carried,[213] shall be chronicled.[214]
If you have any pity, grace, or manners,
You would not make me such an argument.[215]
But fare ye well. 'Tis partly my own fault,
Which death or absence soon shall remedy.
245   *Lysander*   Stay, gentle Helena. Hear my excuse.

200 indeed
201 afFECsiON
202 except
203 setting on = instigation, urging
204 so in grace as you = as graceful/charming/attractive as you are
205 hung upon = furnished, decorated
206 lucky, favored
207 MIZeRAbel
208 go on, keep it up, continue (perSEver)
209 pretend, forge, falsify (verb)
210 dignified, grave, somber
211 derisive/scornful faces
212 hold . . . up = sustain, maintain
213 conducted
214 written down and preserved, like historical chronicles, through the ages
215 speech

My love, my life, my soul, fair Helena!

Helena   O excellent!

Hermia   Sweet, do not scorn her so.

Demetrius If she cannot entreat, I can compel.

Lysander   Thou canst compel no more than she entreat.

Thy threats have no more strength than her weak prayers.   250

Helen, I love thee – by my life, I do.

I swear by that which I will lose for thee,

To prove him false that says I love thee not.

Demetrius I say I love thee more than he can do.

Lysander   If thou say so, withdraw,[216] and prove it too.   255

Demetrius Quick, come!

Hermia   Lysander, whereto tends[217] all this?

Lysander   Away, you Ethiope![218]

Demetrius   No, no. He'll[219]

Seem[220] to break loose. (*to Lysander*) Take on[221] as you

would[222] follow,

But yet come not. You are a tame[223] man, go![224]

Lysander   (*to Hermia*) Hang off, thou cat, thou burr! Vile thing,   260

let loose,

Or I will shake thee from me like a serpent.

Hermia   Why are you grown so rude? What change is this?

216 come aside, retire (away from the presence of women: "step outside")
217 leads, moves, is heading
218 (black = dirty, foul, baleful, wicked)
219 (an unusual but feasible iambic pentameter line, possibly scanned: aWAY
   you EEthiOPE no NO HE'LL)
220 only seem/appear
221 take on = pretend, behave
222 wish to
223 meek, docile
224 off/out with you!

Sweet love —

Lysander   Thy love! Out, tawny Tartar, out!

Out, loathèd medicine![225] Hated potion,[226] hence![227]

Hermia   Do you not jest?

265 *Helena*   Yes, sooth, and so do you.

Lysander   Demetrius, I will keep my word with thee.

Demetrius I would I had your bond,[228] for I perceive

A weak bond[229] holds you. I'll not trust your word.

Lysander   (*to Demetrius*) What, should I hurt her, strike her, kill her dead?

270   Although I hate her, I'll not harm her so.

Hermia   What, can you do me greater harm than hate?

Hate me! Wherefore?[230] O me, what news,[231] my love?

Am not I Hermia? Are not you Lysander?

I am as fair now as I was erewhile.[232]

275   Since night[233] you loved me, yet since night you left me.

Why, then you left me — O, the gods forbid! —

In earnest, shall I say?

Lysander   Ay, by my life.

And never did desire to see thee more.

Therefore be out of hope, of question, of doubt.

280   Be certain. Nothing truer. 'Tis no jest

---

225 drug, poison
226 a dose (portion) of poison
227 outLOATHed MEDicine HATed POtion HENCE
228 written, signed, and legally enforceable agreement (ordinarily for payment of money)
229 Hermia
230 whereFORE
231 new information/tidings
232 formerly, before
233 since night = when it grew dark, earlier tonight

That I do hate thee, and love Helena.

Hermia O me (*to Helena*), you juggler,[234] you canker
blossom,[235]
You thief of love! What, have you come by night
And stolen my love's heart from him?

Helena   Fine, I'faith![236]

Have you no modesty, no maiden shame,   285
No touch of bashfulness?[237] What, will you tear
Impatient answers from my gentle tongue?
Fie, fie, you counterfeit, you puppet,[238] you!

Hermia Puppet? Why so![239] Ay, that way goes the game.

Now I perceive[240] that she hath made compare   290
Between our statures,[241] she hath urged[242] her height,
And with her personage,[243] her tall personage,
Her height, forsooth, she hath prevailed with him.
And are you grown so high in his esteem,
Because I am so dwarfish and so low?[244]   295
How low am I, thou painted maypole?[245] Speak,
How low am I? I am not yet so low
But that my nails can reach unto thine eyes.

Helena I pray you, though you mock me, gentlemen,

234 jester, buffoon, trickster (JUGeLER)
235 flower-consuming worm/caterpillar
236 fine, I'faith = come to an end/be finished/stop!
237 shyness, sensitive modesty
238 (1) dressed-up doll, (2) marionette
239 why so = aha, so that's how it is!
240 understand, comprehend
241 heights
242 advocated, pleaded, pressed
243 appearance, body image, height
244 little, short
245 painted maypole = facially artificially colored skinny person

300 Let her not hurt me. I was never curst,[246]
I have no gift at all in shrewishness.[247]
I am a right[248] maid, for my cowardice.
Let her not strike me. You perhaps may think,
Because she is something lower than myself,
That I can match her.

305 *Hermia*   Lower? Hark, again.

Helena Good Hermia, do not be so bitter with me,
I evermore[249] did love you, Hermia,
Did ever keep your counsels, never wronged you,
Save that, in love unto[250] Demetrius,

310 I told him of your stealth[251] unto[252] this wood.
He followed you; for love I followed him.
But he hath chid[253] me hence and threatened me
To strike me, spurn me, nay, to kill me, too.
And now, so[254] you will let me quiet[255] go,

315 To Athens will I bear my folly back,
And follow you no further. Let me go.
You see how simple[256] and how fond I am.

Hermia Why, get you gone. Who is't that hinders[257] you?

Helena A foolish heart, that I leave here behind.

246 detestable, abominable, virulent, shrewish
247 being ill-tempered / ill-natured / scolding
248 upright, good, proper
249 always
250 with, for
251 furtive / secret going
252 to, into
253 driven me away, with his scolding
254 if thus / therefore, accordingly
255 peacefully, soundlessly
256 harmless, innocent, honest
257 prevents, delays, obstructs

Hermia	What, with Lysander?	
Helena	With Demetrius.	320
Lysander	Be not afraid. She shall not harm thee, Helena.	
Demetrius	No sir. She shall not, though you take her part.	
Helena	O, when she's angry, she is keen and shrewd.[258]	

She was a vixen[259] when she went to school.

And though she be but little, she is fierce.   325

Hermia   Little again? Nothing but low and little?

Why will you suffer[260] her to flout me thus?

Let me come to her.

Lysander   Get you gone, you dwarf,

You minimus,[261] of hindering knot-grass made,[262]

You bead,[263] you acorn.[264]

Demetrius   You are too officious,[265]   330

In her behalf that scorns your services.

Let her alone. Speak not of Helena,

Take not her part. For if thou dost intend

Never so little[266] show of love to her,

Thou shalt aby it.

Lysander   Now she[267] holds me not.   335

---

258 keen and shrewd = fierce and malicious
259 woman who is ill-tempered/quarrelsome/shrewish/fierce-tongued
260 tolerate, allow
261 smallest of small/insignificant creatures
262 of hindering knot-grass made = made of a knotty-stemmed creeping
    weed, the flowers of which, steeped in boiling water, were thought to
    hinder/stunt growth (hindering: an adjective, here)
263 small perforated ball
264 oval nut, seed fruit of the oak tree
265 attentive, eager to please, zealous, meddlesome
266 never so little = the very faintest degree/amount of
267 Hermia

Now follow, if thou dar'st, to try[268] whose right,

Of thine or mine,[269] is most[270] in Helena.

Demetrius Follow? Nay, I'll go with thee, cheek by jowl.[271]

EXEUNT LYSANDER AND DEMETRIUS

Hermia   You, mistress, all this coil[272] is long [273] of you.

Nay, go not back.

340 *Helena*   I will not trust you, I,

Nor longer stay in your curst company.

Your hands than mine are quicker for a fray.

My legs are longer though, to run away.

EXIT HELENA

Hermia   I am amazed, and know not what to say.

EXIT HERMIA

345 *Oberon*   This is thy negligence. Still[274] thou mistak'st,

Or else committ'st[275] thy knaveries willfully.[276]

Puck   Believe me, king of shadows,[277] I mistook.

Did not you tell me I should know the man

By the Athenian garments he had on?

268 find out, test, determine★
269 of thine or mine = yours or mine
270 the greatest
271 cheek by jowl = side by side
272 fuss, confusion, disturbance
273 on account/because of, owing to
274 constantly, continuously, ever, always
275 you perform
276 or ELSE coMITT'ST thy KNAveries WILfulLY
277 unreal appearances, spirits

And so far[278] blameless proves[279] my enterprise[280]   350
That I have 'nointed[281] an Athenian's eyes.
And so far am I glad it so[282] did sort[283]
As this their jangling[284] I esteem[285] a sport.
Oberon Thou see'st, these lovers seek a place to fight.
Hie[286] therefore, Robin, overcast[287] the night,   355
The starry welkin[288] cover thou anon,
With drooping[289] fog as black as Acheron,[290]
And lead these testy[291] rivals so astray
As one come not within another's way.
Like to[292] Lysander sometime frame thy tongue.[293]   360
Then stir Demetrius up with bitter wrong.[294]
And sometime rail[295] thou like Demetrius.
And from each other look thou lead them thus,
Till o'er their brows death-counterfeiting sleep,

278 so far = to that extent
279 is demonstrated/established/shown
280 action, undertaking
281 anointed
282 thus
283 turn out
284 wrangling, quarreling, noisy argument
285 think highly of, account
286 hurry
287 darken
288 arch/vault of heaven ("sky")
289 hanging, descending, sinking
290 hell, the infernal regions
291 irritable, peevish, short-tempered
292 like to = just like
293 frame thy tongue = produce/make your voice/speech
294 unfairness, mischief, transgression
295 rage

365 With leaden legs and batty[296] wings, doth creep.

Then crush[297] this herb into Lysander's eye,

Whose liquor[298] hath this virtuous property,[299]

To take from thence all error with his[300] might,

And make his[301] eyeballs roll with wonted sight.[302]

370 When they next wake, all this derision

Shall seem a dream and fruitless vision,[303]

And back to Athens shall the lovers wend,[304]

With league[305] whose date[306] till death shall never end.

Whiles I in this affair do thee employ,

375 I'll to my queen and beg her Indian boy,

And then I will her charmèd[307] eye release

From monster's view,[308] and all things shall be peace.[309]

Puck My fairy lord, this must be done with haste,

For night's swift dragons[310] cut[311] the clouds full fast,

380 And yonder shines Aurora's harbinger,[312]

296 batlike
297 squeeze
298 liquid ("fluid")
299 virtuous property = natural/inherent power/quality (PROperTIE)
300 its
301 Lysander's
302 roll with wonted sight = move/turn with their usual/customary faculty of
    seeing/eyesight
303 (the rhyme here is deRIZeeON/VIZeeON)
304 return, go off, depart
305 alliance, covenant ("marriage")
306 duration, term
307 enchanted, bewitched
308 monster's view = the seeing/beholding, visual appearance of a monster
309 peaceful (adjective)
310 night's swift dragons = the dragons that pull so rapidly the chariot of Night
311 cut through, break up, dissolve
312 Aurora's harbinger = the dawn's forerunner (the morning star)

At whose approach, ghosts wand'ring here and there
Troop[313] home to churchyards. Damnèd spirits all,[314]
That in crossways[315] and floods[316] have burial,[317]
Already to their wormy[318] beds are gone.
For fear lest day should look their shames[319] upon,   385
They willfully[320] themselves exile[321] from light,
And must for aye consort[322] with black-browed[323] night.
Oberon But we are spirits of another sort.
I with the morning's love[324] have oft made sport,
And, like a forester,[325] the groves may tread[326]   390
Even till[327] the eastern gate,[328] all fiery red,[329]
Opening on Neptune[330] with fair blessèd beams,
Turns into yellow gold his[331] salt green streams.

---

313 go in company
314 damnèd spirits all = the damned spirits whose bodies do not lie in
    churchyards (consecrated ground)
315 crossroads (where suicides were buried)
316 streams, lakes, seas (the dead having drowned and their bodies still lying
    underwater)
317 (burial after a fashion, but not the true, good burial)
318 worm-eaten
319 disgrace, baseness, wickedness
320 voluntarily, deliberately, submissively
321 egZILE (verb)
322 associate, keep company
323 black-browed = frowning, scowling
324 warm affection, kindness (that is, he takes pleasure in the coming of the
    warm sun, and its joyous light)
325 one who supervises/maintains forests/woodlands
326 walk along/in
327 until, the time when
328 (1) entrance, (2) road, path
329 blazing red with dawn (even TILL the EASTern GATE all FIEry RED)
330 opening on Neptune = spreading/expanding/widening out onto the sea/
    ocean
331 the sea's/ocean's

But notwithstanding,[332] haste,[333] make no delay:
395   We may effect this business, yet ere day.

EXIT OBERON

Puck   Up and down, up and down,
    I will lead them up and down.
    I am feared in field and town:
    Goblin, lead them up and down.

ENTER LYSANDER

400   Here comes one.
    Lysander   Where art thou, proud Demetrius? Speak thou now.
    Puck   Here, villain,[334] drawn[335] and ready. Where art thou?
    Lysander   I will be with thee straight.[336]
    Puck   Follow me, then,
    To plainer[337] ground.

EXIT LYSANDER

ENTER DEMETRIUS

Demetrius   Lysander, speak again.
405   Thou runaway, thou coward, art thou fled?
    Speak! In[338] some bush? Where dost thou hide thy head?
    Puck   Thou coward, art thou bragging to the stars,
    Telling the bushes that thou look'st for wars,

332 nevertheless
333 (verb)
334 low-born, base-minded, unprincipled scoundrel
335 my sword drawn from its scabbard
336 directly, immediately
337 flatter, smoother
338 are you in

And wilt not come? Come, recreant,[339] come,[340] thou child,
I'll whip thee with a rod.[341] He[342] is defiled[343]   410
That draws a sword on thee.
Demetrius   Yea,[344] art thou there?
Puck   Follow my voice. We'll try no manhood here.

EXEUNT PUCK AND DEMETRIUS

ENTER LYSANDER

Lysander   He goes before me and still dares me on.
    When I come where he calls, then he is gone.
    The villain is much lighter heeled than I: 415
    I followed fast, but faster he did fly,
    That fallen[345] am I in dark uneven[346] way,
    And here will rest me.

HE LIES DOWN

                    Come, thou gentle day,
    For if but once thou show me thy gray light,
    I'll find Demetrius, and revenge this spite.   420

HE SLEEPS

ENTER PUCK AND DEMETRIUS

339 coward, faint-hearted
340 come RECreeant COME
341 stick
342 any man
343 dishonored, tainted, made dirty
344 all right, yes
345 that fallen = so that come/caught by chance
346 rugged, irregular

Puck	Ho, ho, ho! Coward, why com'st thou not?[347]
Demetrius	Abide[348] me, if thou dar'st, for well I wot[349]

      Thou runn'st before me, shifting every place,[350]

      And dar'st not stand, nor look me in the face.

      Where art thou now?

425 *Puck*   Come hither. I am here.

Demetrius Nay then thou mock'st me. Thou shalt buy this dear,

      If ever I thy face by daylight see.

      Now, go thy way. Faintness constraineth[351] me

      To measure out my length[352] on this cold bed.[353]

· HE LIES DOWN

430   By day's approach look to be visited.[354]

HE SLEEPS

ENTER HELENA

Helena   O weary night, O long and tedious night,

      Abate[355] thy hours, shine comforts[356] from the east,

      That I may back[357] to Athens, by daylight,

      From these that my poor company detest.

435   And sleep, that sometimes shuts up sorrow's eye,

347 HO ho HO COWard why COMST thou NOT
348 wait for
349 know
350 shifting every place = constantly changing your location
351 faintness constraineth = exhaustion forces/compels
352 measure out my length = fall prostrate, lie face down
353 (the ground)
354 look to be visited = expect that you (Lysander) will be dealt with/tested
355 reduce, diminish, lessen
356 encouragement, aid, relief
357 go back, return

Steal me awhile from mine own company.

SHE LIES DOWN AND SLEEPS

Puck   Yet but[358] three? Come one more,
Two of both kinds make up four.
Here she comes, curst[359] and sad.

ENTER HERMIA

Cupid is a knavish lad,   440
Thus to make poor females mad.
Hermia Never so weary, never so in woe,
Bedabbled[360] with the dew and torn with briers.
I can no further crawl, no further go.
My legs can keep no pace[361] with my desires.   445
Here will I rest me till the break of day.

SHE LIES DOWN

Heavens shield Lysander, if they mean a fray![362]

SHE SLEEPS

Puck   On the ground
Sleep sound.
I'll apply   450
To your eye,
Gentle lover, remedy.

---

358 yet but = still only
359 blasted, confused, put to shame
360 wet/made untidy with dirty liquid
361 speed/rate of stepping/walking/going
362 HEAVens SHIELD lysANDer if they MEAN a FRAY

HE SQUEEZES JUICE ON LYSANDER'S EYES

When thou wak'st

Thou tak'st

455   True delight

In the sight

Of thy former lady's eye.

And the country[363] proverb known,[364]

That every man should take his own,

460   In your waking shall be shown.

Jack shall have Jill.

Nought shall go ill.

The man shall have his mare again,[365] and all shall be well.

EXIT PUCK

---

363 rural, rustic

364 familiar, generally recognized

365 (*OED,* mare, 1b, cites as a proverbial phrase a pair of lines by Alexander
Scott, dated 1562: "The heidismen hes 'cor mundam' in thair mouth, / Bot
nevir wt mynd to gif the man his meir" [The headmen/chiefs/leaders have
the world's heart/soul in their mouth/on their tongues, but are not smart
enough to give the man his mare])

Act 4

SCENE I

Lysander, Demetrius, Helena, and Hermia,
still sleeping

enter Titania and Bottom; Peaseblossom,
Cobweb, Moth, Mustardseed, and other Fairies;
and Oberon behind, unseen

Titania Come sit thee down upon this flowery bed,
  While I thy amiable[1] cheeks do coy,[2]
  And stick musk roses in thy sleek[3] smooth head,
  And kiss thy fair large ears, my gentle joy.[4]

Bottom Where's Peaseblossom? 5

Peaseblossom Ready.

Bottom Scratch my head, Peaseblossom. Where's
  Mounsieur Cobweb?

Cobweb Ready.

---

1 lovable, lovely (AIMiyABel)
2 stroke, caress
3 having close-lying hair
4 source of joy

10 *Bottom*   Mounsieur Cobweb, good mounsieur, get you
your weapons in your hand, and kill me a red-hipped
humblebee[5] on the top of a thistle.[6] And good mounsieur,
bring me the honey bag.[7] Do not fret yourself too much in
the action,[8] mounsieur. And good mounsieur, have a care
15 the honey bag break not. I would be loath to have you
overflown[9] with a honey bag, signior. Where's Mounsieur
Mustardseed?

Mustardseed Ready.

Bottom   Give me your neaf,[10] Mounsieur Mustardseed.
20 Pray you, leave your courtesy,[11] good mounsieur.

Mustardseed What's your will?

Bottom   Nothing, good mounsieur, but to help Cavalery[12]
Cobweb to scratch. I must to[13] the barber's, mounsieur, for
methinks I am marvelous hairy about the face, and I am such
25 a tender ass, if my hair do but tickle me, I must scratch.

Titania   What, wilt thou hear some music, my sweet love?

Bottom   I have a reasonable good ear in music. Let's have the
tongs and the bones.[14]

Titania   Or say, sweet love, what thou desirest to eat.

---

5 red-hipped humblebee = a large bee with red hips (up to his hips in the red
clover which, because of their size, only this species of bee can obtain?)

6 purple-flowered prickly plant

7 (not a bag, but an enlarged alimentary canal in which the bee stores up honey)

8 the action = so doing

9 covered, overspread

10 give me your neaf = lend me the use of your clenched hand, fist

11 leave your courtesy = quit/stop your bowing/obeisance

12 Cavalery = gentleman, knight (Italian *cavaliere*)

13 go to

14 tongs . . . bones = percussion instruments (the former = tongs struck by a
smaller bit of metal, the latter = clappers, usually wood, held between the
fingers and rattled against one another)

Bottom Truly, a peck[15] of provender.[16] I could munch your   30
    good dry oats. Methinks I have a great desire to[17] a bottle[18]
    of hay. Good hay, sweet hay, hath no fellow.[19]

Titania I have a venturous[20] fairy that shall seek
    The squirrel's hoard, and fetch thee new[21] nuts.[22]

Bottom I had rather have a handful or two of dried peas. But I   35
    pray you, let none of your people stir[23] me. I have an
    exposition[24] of sleep come upon me.

Titania Sleep thou, and I will wind thee in my arms.
    Fairies, begone, and be all ways away.[25]

EXEUNT FAIRIES

So doth the woodbine the sweet honeysuckle   40
Gently entwist. The female ivy so
Enrings[26] the barky fingers[27] of the elm.
O how I love thee! How I dote on thee!

THEY SLEEP

ENTER PUCK

15 one quarter of a bushel (used for dry foods, usually grain)
16 food, usually fodder (corn, oats)
17 for
18 bundle
19 equal, match
20 daring, bold, adventuresome
21 from the new crop, fresh, not stale
22 the SQUIR.elz HOard AND fetch THEE new NUTS
23 move, shake, disturb
24 (a mangling of "disposition")
25 all ways away = at a distance in every direction
26 encircles, rings around
27 barky fingers = bark-covered foliage/branches/twigs

Oberon Welcome, good Robin. See'st thou this sweet sight?

45   Her dotage[28] now I do begin to pity.

For meeting her of late behind the wood,

Seeking sweet favors from this hateful fool,

I did upbraid[29] her, and fall out with her,

For she his hairy temples then had rounded[30]

50   With coronet[31] of fresh and fragrant flowers.[32]

And that same dew, which sometime on the buds

Was wont to swell like round and orient[33] pearls,

Stood now within the pretty flowerets' eyes

Like tears that did their own disgrace bewail.[34]

55   When I had at my pleasure[35] taunted her,

And she, in mild terms, begged my patience,[36]

I then did ask of her her changeling child,

Which straight she gave me, and her fairy sent

To bear him to my bower in fairy land.

60   And now[37] I have the boy, I will undo

This hateful imperfection of[38] her eyes.

And gentle Puck, take this transformèd scalp[39]

From off the head of this Athenian swain,[40]

28 folly, infatuation
29 reproach, reprove
30 encircled, surrounded
31 a wreath/garland
32 with CORoNET of FRESH and FRAgrant FLOWers
33 oriental
34 disgrace bewail = dishonor/degradation lament/mourn (for having to
    ornament so repulsive a head)
35 at my pleasure = at will/as I pleased/to my satisfaction
36 indulgence, toleration
37 now that
38 imperfection of = blemish in
39 head
40 man of low degree, servant

That he awaking when the other[41] do
May all to Athens back again repair,[42]   65
And think no more of this night's accidents[43]
But as the fierce vexation[44] of a dream.
But first I will release the fairy queen.

Be as thou wast wont to be.
See as thou wast wont to see.   70
Dian's bud, o'er Cupid's flower,
Hath such force and blessèd power.[45]
Now, my Titania, wake you, my sweet queen.
Titania (*waking*) My Oberon, what visions have I seen!
Methought I was enamored of an ass.   75
Oberon There lies your love.
Titania   How came these things to pass?
O how mine eyes do loathe his visage now!
Oberon Silence awhile. Robin, take off this head.
Titania, music call, and strike more dead
Than common sleep of all these five[46] the sense.[47]   80
Titania Music, ho music, such as charmeth sleep.

SUBDUED MUSIC

Puck (*to Bottom, as the ass' head is removed*) Now when thou

41 others
42 go, return
43 happenings
44 harassment, distress, annoyance
45 (not botanically accurate – but who cares?)
46 the four young lovers and Bottom
47 strike more dead ... the sense = make these sleepers' sleep more like
   unbreakable death than ordinary sleep

wak'st, with thine own fool's eyes peep.[48]

Oberon   Sound,[49] music! Come, my queen, take hands with me,

85   And rock the ground[50] whereon these sleepers be.

     Now thou and I are new in amity,

     And will tomorrow midnight solemnly[51]

     Dance in Duke Theseus' house triumphantly,[52]

     And bless it to all[53] fair prosperity.

90   There shall the pairs of faithful lovers be

     Wedded, with Theseus, all in jollity.

Puck   Fairy king, attend, and mark.

     I do hear the morning lark.

Oberon   Then, my queen, in silence sad,[54]

95   Trip[55] we after[56] the night's shade.

     We the globe can compass[57] soon,

     Swifter than the wand'ring[58] moon.

Titania   Come, my lord, and in our flight,

     Tell me how it came this night,

100   That I sleeping here was found,

     With these mortals on the ground.

EXEUNT

---

48 look, see
49 resound
50 rock the ground = shake the ground (by dancing)
51 ceremoniously
52 magnificently, splendidly, nobly
53 the greatest possible
54 orderly, dignified (spelled "sade," as it often was, the rhyme with "shade" becomes comprehensible)
55 prance, skip
56 behind, in pursuit of
57 go round
58 roaming, rambling, irregular

ACT 4 · SCENE I

ENTER THESEUS, HIPPOLYTA, EGEUS, AND TRAIN,
TO THE SOUND OF HORNS

Theseus   Go, one of you, find out[59] the forester.
For now our observation[60] is performed.
And since we have the vaward[61] of the day,
My love shall hear the music of my hounds.   105
Uncouple[62] in the western valley, let them go.
Dispatch,[63] I say, and find the forester.

EXIT ATTENDANT

We will, fair queen, up[64] to the mountain's top,
And mark the musical confusion[65]
Of hounds and echo in conjunction.[66]   110
Hippolyta I was with Hercules and Cadmus[67] once,
When in a wood of Crete they bayed[68] the bear,
With hounds of Sparta. Never did I hear
Such gallant chiding,[69] for besides the groves,
The skies, the fountains,[70] every region[71] near   115

59 find out = locate
60 observance of custom, law (in celebrating Midsummer's Eve)
61 vanguard, front rank
62 free the hounds from their leashes
63 hurry (verb)
64 go up
65 blending, intermixing, fusion (conFYUSiON)
66 conDJUNKsiyON
67 Hercules = son of Zeus and Alkmena; Cadmus = legendary founder of
     Thebes
68 pursued and trapped by hounds' baying/barking
69 gallant chiding = excellent/splendid/grand angry noise/brawling (used of
     foxhounds)
70 springs
71 tract of land ("place")

Seemed all one mutual cry.[72] I never heard
So musical a discord,[73] such sweet thunder.[74]

Theseus My hounds are bred out of the Spartan kind,[75]
So flewed, so sanded.[76] And their heads are hung
120 With ears that sweep away the morning dew,
Crook-kneed, and dewlapped[77] like Thessalian[78] bulls –
Slow in pursuit, but matched in mouth like bells,
Each under each.[79] A cry[80] more tuneable[81]
Was never holla'd[82] to, nor cheered with[83] horn,
125 In Crete, in Sparta, nor in Thessaly.
Judge when you hear. (*seeing Hermia, Helena, Lysander,
Demestrius, sleeping*)

But soft! What nymphs are these?

Egeus   My lord, this is my daughter here asleep,
And this, Lysander; this Demetrius is;
130 This Helena, old Nedar's Helena.
I wonder of[84] their being here together.

Theseus No doubt they rose up early, to observe

---

72 mutual cry = reciprocal/common animal vocal utterance
73 diversity, mingling
74 loud/resounding noise
75 descent, race
76 so flewed, so sanded = just-so large-jawed (like bloodhounds), just-so sand-colored
77 crook-kneed and dewlapped = crooked/bent-kneed and with loose skin hanging from their throats
78 Thessaly: rich agricultural region in northern Greece
79 (that is, in pitch)
80 pack
81 well-tuned, harmonious, melodious
82 to call to hounds
83 cheered with = enouraged/encited/animated by
84 wonder of = am astonished at/by

The rite of May. And hearing our intent,
Came here in grace[85] of our solemnity.
But speak, Egeus, is not this the day   135
That Hermia should[86] give answer of her choice?[87]

Egeus   It is, my lord.

Theseus   Go, bid the huntsmen wake them with their horns.

SHOUTS AND HORNS WITHIN

LYSANDER, DEMETRIUS, HELENA, AND HERMIA WAKE

Good morrow,[88] friends. Saint Valentine[89] is past.
Begin these woodbirds but to couple[90] now?   140

LYSANDER, DEMETRIUS, HELENA, AND HERMIA KNEEL

Lysander Pardon,[91] my lord.

Theseus   I pray you all, stand up.
I know you two are rival enemies.[92]
How comes this gentle concord[93] in the world,
That hatred is so far from jealousy[94]
To sleep by[95] hate, and fear no enmity?[96]   145

85 honor
86 must
87 that HERmya SHOULD give ANswer OF her CHOICE
88 good morrow = good morning
89 February = St. Valentine's Day (when birds were supposed to choose their
   mates)
90 join in marriage, link together, connect
91 we beg your pardon
92 rival enemies = competing adversaries/antagonists
93 harmony, agreement
94 anger, suspicion, mistrust
95 near, beside
96 ill will, hostility

Lysander My lord, I shall[97] reply amazedly,[98]
          Half sleep, half waking. But, as yet, I swear,
          I cannot truly say how I came here.
          But as I think – for truly would I speak,
150   And now do I bethink me, so it is –
          I came with Hermia hither. Our intent
          Was to be gone from Athens, where we might,
          Without[99] the peril of the Athenian law –
Egeus   Enough, enough, my lord. You have enough.
155   I beg the law, the law, upon his head.
          (*to Demetrius*) They would have stol'n away, they would,
          Demetrius,
          Thereby to have defeated[100] you and me:
          You of your wife, and me of my consent,
          Of my consent that she should be your wife.
160 *Demetrius* My lord, fair Helen told me of their stealth,
          Of this their purpose hither[101] to this wood,
          And I in fury hither followed them,
          Fair Helena in fancy[102] following me.
          But my good lord, I wot not by what power[103] –
165   But by some power it is – my love to Hermia,
          Melted as the snow, seems to me now
          As the remembrance of an idle gaud[104]

  97 must
  98 in bewilderment, consternation, astonishment
  99 outside, beyond
 100 frustrated, cheated
 101 in coming here
 102 amorous inclination, love
 103 source of external influence / control
 104 plaything, toy

Which in my childhood I did dote upon.
And all the faith, the virtue[105] of my heart,
The object and the pleasure of mine eye,   170
Is only Helena. To her, my lord,
Was I betrothed, ere I saw Hermia.
But, like a sickness, did I loathe this food.[106]
But, as in health, come to my natural taste,[107]
Now I do wish it, love it, long for it,   175
And will for evermore be true to it.

Theseus   Fair lovers, you are fortunately met.
Of this discourse[108] we more will hear anon.
Egeus, I will overbear[109] your will:
For in the temple, by and by, with us   180
These couples shall eternally be knit.
And, for[110] the morning now is something worn,[111]
Our purposed[112] hunting shall be set aside.
Away, with us, to Athens. Three and three,
We'll hold a feast, in great solemnity.   185
Come, Hippolyta.

EXEUNT THESEUS, HIPPOLYTA, EGEUS, AND TRAIN

Demetrius   These things seem small and undistinguishable,
Like far-off mountains turned into clouds.

105 worth
106 nourishment (used figuratively)
107 discernment, perception, judgment
108 narration, tale (noun)
109 put down, outweigh
110 because
111 something worn = somewhat/to a certain extent spent/exhausted
112 intended

Hermia   Methinks I see these things with parted[113] eye,
When every thing seems double.

190 *Helena*   So methinks.
And I have found Demetrius like a jewel,
Mine own, and not mine own.

Demetrius   Are you sure
That we are awake?[114] It seems to me
That yet we sleep, we dream. Do not you think

195 The Duke was here, and bid us follow him?

Hermia   Yea, and my father.

Helena   And Hippolyta.

Lysander   And he did bid us follow to the temple.

Demetrius   Why, then we are awake. Let's follow him,
And by[115] the way let us recount[116] our dreams.

EXEUNT

200 *Bottom*   (*waking*) When my cue comes, call me, and I will
answer. My next[117] is, "Most fair Pyramus." Heigh-ho! Peter
Quince? Flute, the bellowsmender? Snout, the tinker?
Starveling? God's my life, stolen hence, and left me asleep! I
have had a most rare vision. I have had a dream, past the wit

205 of man to say what dream it was. Man is but an ass, if he go
about to expound[118] this dream. Methought I was – there is
no man can tell what. Methought I was – and methought I

---

113 divided ("double vision")
114 THAT we ARE aWAKE
115 along
116 narrate, give a full account of
117 next line
118 explain, interpret

had — but man is but a patch'd fool,[119] if he will offer[120] to
say what methought I had. The eye of man hath not heard,
the ear of man hath not seen, man's hand is not able to taste,   210
his tongue to conceive, nor his heart to report,[121] what my
dream was. I will get Peter Quince to write a ballad[122] of this
dream. It shall be called "Bottom's Dream," because it hath no
bottom.[123] And I will sing it in the latter end[124] of a play,
before the Duke. Peradventure,[125] to make it the more   215
gracious,[126] I shall sing it at her[127] death.

EXIT

119 patched fool = a fool/clown wearing a coat made of patches (particolored
    bits of cloth)
120 propose, volunteer, try
121 (a mangling of the Bible, 1 Cor. 2:9: "Eye hath not seen, nor ear heard,
    neither have entered into the heart of man, the things which God hath
    prepared for them that love him")
122 printed sheet of a song, set to a familiar melody, celebrating/attacking
    someone/something
123 hath no bottom = is unfathomable/inexhaustible
124 latter end = concluding part
125 perchance, perhaps
126 acceptable, pleasing, likely to find favor
127 Thisbe's (in the workmen's play)

SCENE 2

Athens. Quince's house

ENTER QUINCE, FLUTE, SNOUT, AND STARVELING

Quince   Have you sent[1] to Bottom's house? Is he come home yet?

Starveling He cannot be heard of.[2] Out of doubt he is transported.[3]

5 *Flute*   If he come not, then the play is marred.[4] It goes not forward,[5] doth it?

Quince   It is not possible. You have not a man in all Athens able to discharge[6] Pyramus but he.

Flute   No, he hath simply the best wit of any handicraft
10   man[7] in Athens.

Quince   Yea, and the best person,[8] too, and he is a very paramour[9] for a sweet voice.

Flute   You must say paragon.[10] A paramour is, God bless us, a thing of naught.[11]

ENTER SNUG, THE WOODWORKER

15 *Snug*   Masters, the Duke is coming from the temple, and there

1 a message/messenger
2 cannot be heard of = nothing can be learned/there is no word/information about him
3 is transported = has been carried off (presumably by the fairies)
4 spoiled, useless
5 ahead
6 perform, acquit oneself of
7 handicraft man = artisan, skilled workman
8 appearance, figure, body
9 illicit/secret lover (a mangling that Quince promptly corrects)
10 model/pattern of excellence
11 wickedness, evil, moral wrong

is two or three lords and ladies more[12] married. If our sport
had gone forward, we had all been made men.[13]

Flute   O sweet bully Bottom! Thus hath he lost sixpence a day
during his life.[14] He could not have 'scaped[15] sixpence a day.
And[16] the Duke had not given him sixpence a day for playing   20
Pyramus, I'll be hanged.[17] He would have deserved it.
Sixpence a day in [18] Pyramus, or nothing.[19]

ENTER BOTTOM

Bottom   Where are these lads?[20] Where are these hearts?[21]

Quince   Bottom! O most courageous[22] day! O most happy hour!

Bottom   Masters, I am to discourse[23] wonders. But ask me not   25
what. For if I tell you, I am no true Athenian. I will[24] tell you
everything right as it fell out.

Quince   Let us hear, sweet Bottom.

Bottom   Not a word of[25] me. All that I will tell you is, that the

12 in addition
13 made men = men of assured success/prosperity
14 (that is, a pension would be given him as a reward: by the wage scales of the
   time, sixpence per day is roughly twice what most of these men regularly
   earned)
15 avoided
16 if
17 I'll be hanged = I'll be damned
18 sixpence a day in Pyramus = there is/ought to be sixpence a day in playing
   Pyramus
19 (Flute's angry, insistent vehemence suggests that he might have been
   drinking, especially since at this point, with Bottom apparently unavailable,
   the likelihood is that nothing will be received for playing Pyramus)
20 fellows
21 spirited/courageous fellows
22 brave, splendid
23 I am to discourse = I will speak/narrate/tell (verb)
24 will in the future
25 from

30   Duke hath dined.[26] Get your apparel[27] together, good strings
to[28] your beards, new ribbons to your pumps,[29] meet
presently[30] at the palace, every man look o'er his part. For the
short and the long is, our play is preferred.[31] In any case, let
Thisbe have clean linen,[32] and let not him that plays the lion
35   pare[33] his nails, for they shall[34] hang out for the lion's claws.
And most dear actors, eat no onions nor garlic. For we are to
utter sweet breath. And I do not doubt but to hear them say, it
is a sweet comedy. No more words. Away, go away.[35]

EXEUNT

26 (that is, it is now after dinnertime, and their play will called for)
27 clothing, costumes (perhaps props, as well)
28 for tying them on
29 (low-heeled shoes for dancing, acrobatics, etc., often decorated with ribbons)
30 promptly, directly, quickly
31 approved, desired, put forward
32 underwear
33 trim
34 must
35 away, go away = move, go along

Act 5

SCENE I

Theseus' palace, Athens

ENTER THESEUS, HIPPOLYTA, PHILOSTRATE,
LORDS, AND ATTENDANTS

Hippolyta 'Tis strange my Theseus, that[1] these lovers speak of.
Theseus   More strange than true. I never may[2] believe
  These antique fables,[3] nor these fairy toys.[4]
  Lovers and madmen have such seething[5] brains,
  Such shaping[6] fantasies, that apprehend[7]   5
  More than cool reason ever comprehends.
  The lunatic, the lover, and the poet

1 that which
2 can
3 antique fables = old/old-fashioned legendary/mythological fiction,
  falsehoods, nonsense
4 idle/fantastic tales
5 boiling, tumultuous, ceaselessly agitated
6 formative/creative
7 learn, perceive, understand, become conscious of

Are of imagination all compact.[8]
One sees more devils than vast hell can hold:
10   That is the madman. The lover, all[9] as frantic,[10]
Sees Helen's beauty in a brow of Egypt.[11]
The poet's eye, in a fine frenzy,[12] rolling,
Doth glance from heaven to earth, from earth to heaven.
And as imagination bodies forth[13]
15   The forms of things unknown, the poet's pen
Turns them to shapes and gives to airy nothing
A local habitation,[14] and a name.
Such tricks[15] hath strong imagination,[16]
That[17] if it would but[18] apprehend some joy,
20   It comprehends[19] some bringer of that joy.
Or[20] in the night, imagining some fear,
How easy is a bush supposed a bear?

Hippolyta   But all the story of the night told over,[21]
And all their minds transfigured[22] so together,
25   More witnesseth[23] than fancy's images,

8 (1) composed, (2) linked closely together
9 every bit
10 wild, raging
11 brow of Egypt = dark/gypsy face
12 fine frenzy = pure/consummate/elevated delirium/mania
13 bodies forth = embodies, gives shape to
14 local habitation = spatial position, dwelling, residence
15 devices, stratagems
16 iMAgiNAsiON
17 so that
18 would but = only
19 grasps, understands
20 in the same way
21 (1) repeatedly, (2) as a whole, fully
22 altered, changed
23 testifies to, attests, provides evidence for

> And grows to something of great constancy.[24]
> But howsoever,[25] strange and admirable.[26]

Theseus   Here come the lovers, full of joy and mirth.

ENTER LYSANDER, DEMETRIUS, HERMIA, AND HELENA

> Joy,[27] gentle friends, joy and fresh[28] days of love
> Accompany your hearts.

Lysander   More than to us   30
> Wait[29] in your royal walks,[30] your board,[31] your bed.

Theseus   Come now.[32] What masques,[33] what dances shall we
> have,
> To wear away this long age[34] of three hours,[35]
> Between our after supper and bedtime?
> Where is our usual[36] manager of mirth?   35
> What revels[37] are in hand? Is there no play
> To ease the anguish of a torturing hour?[38]
> Call Philostrate.

Philostrate   Here, mighty Theseus.

24 steadiness, firmness
25 in any case, at any rate
26 strange and admirable = alien/unknown and surprising/wonderful
27 may joy . . .
28 new, additional
29 more than to us wait = may more than we receive await you
30 garden paths
31 food, meals
32 now then
33 (1) masked balls, (2) court entertainments, consisting of music, dancing, and
   some dialogue
34 period, time
35 to WEAR aWAY this LONG age OF three HOURS
36 customary, ordinary, regular
37 festivity, merry making, entertainment
38 a relatively short time, but not precisely an hour

40 *Theseus*   Say, what abridgment[39] have you for this evening?
What masque, what music? How shall we beguile[40]
The lazy[41] time, if not with some delight?
Philostrate (*gives him paper*) There is a brief,[42] how many sports
are ripe.
Make choice, of which your highness will[43] see first.
45 *Theseus*   (*reads*) "The battle with the Centaurs,[44] to be sung
By an Athenian eunuch[45] to the harp?"
We'll[46] none of that. That have I told my love,
In glory[47] of my kinsman Hercules.
"The riot of the tipsy Bacchanals,[48]
50 Tearing the Thracian singer[49] in their rage?"
That is an old device,[50] and it was played
When I from Thebes came last a[51] conqueror.
"The thrice three[52] Muses mourning for the death
Of Learning, late deceased in beggary?"[53]
55 That is some satire, keen and critical,[54]

39 method for shortening time
40 delude, foil, divert
41 slothful, slow moving
42 short list
43 wishes to
44 head, trunk, and arms of a man joined to a horse's body and legs (Hercules
   killed the centaur Nessus, who tried to rape Hercules' wife, but the dying
   centaur tricked Hercules' wife into a scheme that later killed Hercules)
45 castrated male
46 we'll = we'll have
47 honor
48 tipsy Bacchanals = drunken worshippers of Bacchus, god of wine
49 Thracian singer = Orpheus
50 theatrical plot
51 came last a = came the last time as a
52 thrice three = nine
53 extreme poverty
54 keen and critical = harsh/clever and fault-finding

Not sorting with[55] a nuptial ceremony.
"A tedious[56] brief scene of young Pyramus
And his love Thisbe, very tragical mirth?"
Merry and tragical? Tedious and brief?
That is hot ice and wondrous strange snow.   60
How shall we find the concord of this discord?

Philostrate   A play there is, my lord, some ten words long,
Which is as brief as I have known a play.
But by ten words, my lord, it is too long,
Which makes it tedious. For in all the play,   65
There is not one word apt, one player fitted.[57]
And tragical, my noble lord, it is.
For Pyramus therein doth kill himself.
Which, when I saw rehearsed, I must confess,
Made mine eyes water — but more merry tears   70
The passion of loud laughter never shed.

Theseus   What are they, that do play it?

Philostrate Hard-handed men, that work in Athens here,
Which never labored in their minds till now.
And now have toiled[58] their unbreathed[59] memories   75
With this same play, against your nuptial.

Theseus   And we will hear it.

Philostrate No, my noble lord,
It is not for you. I have heard it over,
And it is nothing, nothing in the world,   80

55 sorting with = suitable for, befitting, in harmony with
56 (1) wearisome, (2) long
57 suitable, qualified, competent
58 fatigued, exhausted
59 unpracticed

Unless you can find sport in their intents,
Extremely stretched[60] and conned[61] with cruel pain,
To do you service.

Theseus   I will hear that play,
For never anything can be amiss[62]
85   When simpleness[63] and duty tender it.
Go, bring them in, and take your places, ladies.

EXIT PHILOSTRATE

Hippolyta I love not to see wretchedness[64] o'ercharged,[65]
And duty in his service[66] perishing.[67]
Theseus   Why, gentle sweet, you shall see no such thing.
90   *Hippolyta* He says they can do nothing in this kind.
Theseus   The kinder we, to give them thanks for nothing.
Our sport shall be to take what they mistake.
And what poor duty cannot do, noble respect[68]
Takes it in might, not merit.[69]
95   Where I have come, great clerks[70] have purposèd
To greet me with premeditated[71] welcomes,

---

60 extended, strained
61 studied, memorized
62 wrong, faulty, deficient
63 plain / unassuming manners / disposition, innocence
64 poverty, inferiority
65 overburdened, overloaded, oppressed
66 his service = doing what it must do for its master
67 wasted, squandered
68 perspective, view, regard, consideration
69 in might, not merit = in terms of the capacities / capabilities on display, not
   the worth of what we see
70 churchmen, scholars
71 composed / written out in advance

Where[72] I have seen them shiver and look pale,
Make periods[73] in the midst of sentences,
Throttle[74] their practiced accent[75] in their fears,
And in conclusion[76] dumbly have broke off, 100
Not paying me a welcome. Trust[77] me, sweet,
Out of this silence, yet,[78] I picked[79] a welcome.
And in the modesty of fearful[80] duty
I read as much, as from the rattling[81] tongue
Of saucy and audacious[82] eloquence. 105
Love, therefore, and tongue-tied simplicity
In least[83] speak most, to my capacity.[84]

ENTER PHILOSTRATE

Philostrate So please your Grace, the Prologue[85] is addressed.[86]
Theseus   Let him approach.

FLOURISH OF TRUMPETS

72 in the course of which
73 make periods = make pauses, stop
74 strangle, choke on
75 practiced accent = rehearsed speech
76 in conclusion = finally
77 believe
78 still
79 plucked, gathered, drew
80 frightened, awed
81 rapid-flowing
82 saucy and audacious = presumptuous/cheeky/insolent and confident/
    bold/shameless
83 saying less
84 power to understand/absorb/take in
85 (1) the introductory statement, (2) the person speaking it (the likelier
    meaning, here)
86 ready, prepared

ENTER QUINCE ("PROLOGUE")

110 *Quince*   If we offend, it is with our good will.[87]

That[88] you should think, we come not to offend,

But[89] with good will. To show our simple skill,

That is the true beginning of our end.[90]

Consider[91] then, we come but in despite.[92]

115 We do not come, as minding[93] to content you,

Our true intent is.[94] All for your delight,

We are not here. That you should here repent you,[95]

The actors are at hand. And by their show[96]

You shall know all, that you are like to[97] know.

120 *Theseus*   This fellow doth not stand upon points.[98]

Lysander He hath rid[99] his prologue like a rough[100] colt. He

---

87 with our good will = (1) willingly, (2) we intend well
88 though
89 (1) yet, (2) except
90 (1) conclusion, (2) purpose, (3) death
91 (1) remember, (2) think
92 (1) disdain, scorn, contempt, defiance, (2) indignation, anger, annoyance,
   (3) notwithstanding who and what we are
93 (1) caring, paying attention, (2) remembering, thinking of
94 (Quince is reciting the words as if reading them – and he has the
   punctuation thoroughly fouled up: there should be no period after "is"; the
   comma after "delight" should be a period; there should be no period after
   "here"; the comma after "you" should be a period; the period after "hand"
   should be a comma; and there should be no comma after "all")
95 repent you = be sorry/regret that you are here
96 actions, appearance
97 like to = likely to (Quince is probably meant to say something more like
   "that you might like to know")
98 stand upon points = (1) worry about punctuation, (2) insist on details,
   speak with great care, (3) heights, summits, (4) the squares of a
   chessboard (?)
99 ridden
100 wild, unbroken

knows not the stop.[101] A good moral,[102] my lord. It is not
enough to speak, but to speak[103] true.

Hippolyta Indeed he hath played on his prologue like a child on
a recorder[104] – a sound, but not in government.[105]   125

Theseus   His speech was like a tangled chain, nothing
impaired,[106] but all disordered.[107] Who is next?

ENTER TRUMPETER, FOLLOWED BY BOTTOM ("PYRAMUS")
AND FLUTE ("THISBE"), SNOUT ("WALL"), STARVELING
("MOONSHINE"), AND SNUG ("LION")

Quince   Gentles, perchance you wonder at this show.
But, wonder on, till truth make all things plain.
This man is Pyramus, if you would know.   130
This beauteous lady Thisbe is certain.[108]
This man, with lime and rough-cast, doth present
Wall, that vile Wall which did these lovers sunder.[109]
And through Wall's chink, poor souls, they are content
To whisper. At the which let no man wonder.   135
This man, with lanthorn, dog, and bush of thorn,
Presenteth Moonshine.[110] For, if you will know,
By moonshine did these lovers think[111] no scorn
To meet at Ninus' tomb, there, there to woo.

101 (1) stopping, (2) checking, (3) a period
102 moral teaching / exposition, practical lesson
103 to speak = we must speak
104 wooden flute, played in a vertical rather than a horizontal position
105 in government = under control
106 injured, damaged
107 confused, corrupted
108 without doubt, for sure (serTAIN)
109 separate (verb)
110 (1) moonlight, (2) appearance without substance, foolish talk
111 think it

140   This grisly beast, which Lion hight[112] by name,

The trusty Thisbe, coming first by night,

Did scare away, or rather did affright.

And as she fled, her mantle she did fall,[113]

Which Lion vile with bloody mouth did stain.

145   Anon comes Pyramus, sweet youth, and tall,[114]

And finds his trusty Thisbe's mantle slain.[115]

Whereat, with blade, with bloody blameful[116] blade,

He bravely broached[117] his boiling bloody breast.

And Thisbe, tarrying in mulberry shade,

150   His[118] dagger drew, and died. For all the rest,

Let Lion, Moonshine, Wall, and lovers twain,

At large[119] discourse, while here they do remain.

     EXEUNT QUINCE, BOTTOM, SNUG, AND STARVELING

Theseus   I wonder if the lion be to speak.

Demetrius   No wonder,[120] my lord. One lion may, when many

asses do.

155 *Snout*   In this same interlude it doth befall

That I, one Snout by name, present a wall.

And such a wall, as I would have you think

That had in it a crannied hole or chink,

Through which the lovers, Pyramus and Thisbe,

160   Did whisper often very secretly.

112 is called
113 drop
114 handsome, proper
115 (1) slaughtered, (2) stained (?)
116 disgraceful, scandalous
117 stabbed, pierced, thrust through
118 Pyramus'
119 at large = freely
120 no wonder = nothing to marvel at

This loam, this rough-cast, and this stone doth show,
That I am that same wall. The truth is so.
And this the cranny is, right and sinister,[121]
Through which the fearful lovers are to whisper.

Theseus   Would you desire lime and hair to speak better?   165
Demetrius It is the wittiest partition[122] that ever I heard
discourse, my lord.

ENTER BOTTOM

Theseus   Pyramus draws near the wall. Silence.
Bottom   O grim-looked night, O night with hue so black,
O night, which ever art when day is not.   170
O night, O night, alack, alack, alack,
I fear my Thisbe's promise is forgot.
And thou, O wall, O sweet, O lovely wall,
That stand'st between her father's ground and mine,
Thou wall, O wall, O sweet and lovely wall,   175
Show me thy chink, to blink[123] through with mine eyne!

SNOUT STRETCHES OUT HIS FINGERS

Thanks, courteous Wall. Jove shield thee well, for this.
But what see I? No Thisbe do I see.
O wicked Wall, through whom I see no bliss,
Cursed be thy stones for thus deceiving me.   180
Theseus   The wall, methinks, being sensible,[124] should curse
again.[125]

---

121 right and sinister = right and left
122 wisest/most intelligent (1) structural division, (2) section of a book
123 look
124 capable of feeling and perceiving
125 back

Bottom No, in truth, sir, he should not. "Deceiving me" is
      Thisbe's cue. She is to enter now, and I am to spy her through
185   the wall. You shall see, it will fall pat as I told you. Yonder she
      comes.

ENTER FLUTE

Flute   O wall, full often hast thou heard my moans,
      For parting my fair Pyramus, and me.
      My cherry lips have often kissed thy stones,
190   Thy stones, with lime and hair knit up in thee.[126]
Bottom I see[127] a voice. Now will I to[128] the chink,
      To spy and[129] I can hear my Thisbe's face. Thisbe?
      Thisbe?[130]
Flute   My love thou art, my love I think.[131]
195 *Bottom* Think what thou wilt, I am thy lover's grace.[132]
      And like Limander[133] am I trusty still.[134]
Flute   And I, like Helen,[135] till the Fates me kill.
Bottom Not Shafalus[136] to Procrus[137] was so true.
Flute   As Shafalus to Procrus, I to you.

126 knit up in thee: Folio reading (First Quarto: knit now againe)
127 see . . . voice: Bottom-mangling of language (see *can* mean perceive
      mentally / internally – but in the very next line, hear . . . face eliminates all
      uncertainty)
128 go to
129 if
130 reiteration of the name occurs in the Folio, but not in the First Quarto
131 (this bad poetry rhymes, and bad rhyming poetry often chooses words only
      for their rhyme)
132 the favor that your lover brings you (?)
133 (mangling of Leander, as in Hero [female] and Leander)
134 always
135 (mangling of Hero)
136 (mangling of Cephalus [male])
137 (mangling of Procris [female])

Bottom	O kiss me through the hole of this vile wall!	200
Flute	I kiss the wall's hole,[138] not your lips at all.	
Bottom	Wilt thou at Ninny's[139] tomb meet me straightway?	
Flute	'Tide[140] life, 'tide death, I come without delay.	

EXEUNT BOTTOM AND FLUTE

Snout	Thus have I, Wall, my part dischargèd so,	
	And, being done, thus Wall away doth go.	205

EXIT SNOUT

Theseus   Now is the mural[141] down between the two neighbors.

Demetrius No remedy, my lord, when walls are so willful to[142] hear without warning.[143]

Hippolyta This is the silliest stuff that ever I heard.   210

Theseus   The best in this kind[144] are but shadows,[145] and the worst are no worse,[146] if imagination amend them.

Hippolyta It must be your imagination then, and not theirs.

Theseus   If we imagine no worse of them than they of themselves, they may pass for excellent men. Here come two   215
noble beasts in, a man and a lion.

138 (1) chink, (2) anus
139 (Ninus mangled, once again)
140 betide: happen, come
141 wall (in the 15th and 16th centuries, "mure" and "mural" are synonymous with "wall")
142 as to
143 (cautioning that they can hear – since, as has long been said, walls have ears . . .)
144 (that is, theatrical plays)
145 vain, unreal, ephemeral, feeble imitations
146 (that is, no worse than this: a left-handed compliment, this play then being at least no worse than other bad plays)

ENTER SNUG AND STARVELING

Snug	You, ladies, you (whose gentle hearts do fear
	The smallest monstrous[147] mouse that creeps on floor),
	May now, perchance, both quake and tremble here,
220	When lion rough, in wildest rage, doth roar.
	Then know that I, as Snug the joiner, am
	A lion fell,[148] nor else no lion's dam,[149]
	For if I should as lion come in strife
	Into this place, 'twere pity on my life.[150]
225	*Theseus* A very gentle[151] beast, and of a good conscience.[152]
	Demetrius The very best at[153] a beast, my lord, that e'er I saw.
	Lysander This lion is a very fox for his valor.[154]
	Theseus True. And a goose[155] for his discretion.[156]
	Demetrius Not so, my lord. For his valor cannot carry his
230	discretion. And the fox carries the goose.
	Theseus His discretion, I am sure, cannot carry his valor. For
	the goose carries not the fox. It is well. Leave it to his
	discretion, and let us listen to the moon.
	Starveling This lanthorn doth the hornèd moon present –

147 gigantic, monster-sized
148 savage, fierce, cruel
149 I, who am Snug the joiner [woodworker], am here representing a cruel/
    fierce/savage lion, nor am I in any other way a lioness, either
150 'twere pity on my life = it would be a cause for sorrow in my life (that is, he
    would be killed)
151 (see Finding List)
152 of a good conscience = moral, right-thinking
153 as, at being
154 courage, bravery (that is, he's *not* courageous: foxes were notorious for
    running from danger)
155 fool, simpleton
156 judgment, faculty of discernment, sagacity

Demetrius He should have worn the horns on his head.[157] 235

Theseus He is no crescent,[158] and his horns are invisible within the circumference.

Starveling This lanthorn doth the hornèd moon present; Myself the man i' the moon do seem[159] to be.

Theseus This is the greatest error of all the rest. The man 240
should be put into the lanthorn. How is it else the Man i' the Moon?

Demetrius He dares not come there for[160] the candle. For, you see, it is already in snuff.[161]

Hippolyta I am aweary of this moon. Would he would 245
change![162]

Theseus It appears, by his[163] small light of discretion, that he is in the wane.[164] But yet, in courtesy, in all reason,[165] we must stay the time.

Lysander Proceed, Moon. 250

Starveling All that I have to say, is to tell you that the lanthorn is the moon; I, the man in the moon; this thorn bush, my thorn bush; and this dog, my dog.

Demetrius Why? All these should be in the lanthorn, for all these are in the moon. But, silence. Here comes Thisbe. 255

157 (that is, he is a cuckold)
158 (that is, not a crescent or new moon, but a thick full one – though he is *Starveling*)
159 do seem = appear
160 because of
161 in snuff = the accumulated burned wick needs to be cleaned out
162 pass into a new phase (the moon is notoriously changeable)
163 (since his = its, the punning is intensified: the moon's light [illumination] and the man's light [brains])
164 he is in the wane = he/it (moon/man light/brain) is decreasing
165 reasonableness

ENTER THISBE

Thisbe	This is old Ninny's tomb. Where is my love?
Snug	O –

SNUG ROARS. THISBE DROPS HER MANTLE AND RUNS OFF

Demetrius Well roared, Lion.
Theseus Well run, Thisbe.
260 *Hippolyta* Well shone, Moon. Truly, the moon shines with a
good grace.[166]

THE LION WORRIES THISBE'S MANTLE, AND THEN EXITS

Theseus Well moused, Lion.
Demetrius And then came Pyramus –
Lysander And so the lion vanished.

ENTER PYRAMUS

265 *Pyramus* Sweet Moon, I thank thee for thy sunny[167] beams.
I thank thee, Moon, for shining now so bright.
For by thy gracious, golden,[168] glittering gleams,
I trust to take of truest Thisbe sight.
But stay. O spite!
270   But mark, poor knight,
What dreadful dole[169] is here?
Eyes, do you see?
How can it be?
O dainty duck! O dear!

166 with a good grace = willingly, cheerfully
167 Bottom-mangling (sunny = cheerful, joyous, bright; but . . .)
168 (who has ever seen golden moonlight?)
169 crime, sorrow, fate, destiny

Thy mantle good, 275

What, stained with blood?

Approach, ye Furies fell!

O Fates, come, come,

Cut[170] thread and thrum,[171]

Quail,[172] crush, conclude, and quell![173] 280

Theseus This passion, and the death of a dear friend, would go

near[174] to make a man look sad.[175]

Hippolyta Beshrew my heart, but I pity the man.

Pyramus O wherefore, Nature, didst thou lions frame?[176]

Since lion vile hath here deflowered[177] my dear. 285

Which is — no, no — which was the fairest dame[178]

That lived, that loved, that liked, that looked with cheer.[179]

Come, tears, confound,[180]

Out, sword, and wound

The pap[181] of Pyramus; 290

Ay, that left pap,

Where heart doth hop.[182]

HE STABS HIMSELF

170 (one Fate spins life's threads; the second draws it out; the third cuts it)
171 ends of warp threads left on a loom when the weaving net is cut off
172 destroy
173 kill
174 go near to = go close to, almost
175 weary, sorrowful
176 lions frame = make lions
177 ravaged, violated
178 lady (that is, a woman of high social status)
179 with cheer = cheerfully
180 destroy, silence (verb)
181 nipple
182 leap, spring

Thus die I, thus, thus, thus.

Now am I dead,

295   Now am I fled,[183]

My soul is in the sky.

Tongue,[184] lose thy light.

Moon take thy flight.

EXIT STARVELING (MOON)[185]

Now die, die, die, die, die.

HE DIES

300 *Demetrius* No die,[186] but an ace[187] for him, for he is but one.

Lysander Less than an ace man.[188] For he is dead, he is nothing.

Theseus With the help of a surgeon[189] he might yet recover, and prove[190] an ass.

Hippolyta How chance[191] Moonshine is gone before Thisbe

305 comes back and finds her lover?

Theseus She will find him by starlight. Here she comes, and her passion[192] ends the play.

ENTER FLUTE

183 fled from this life ("dead")
184 Bottom-mangling: tongue substituted for eye (?)
185 (the joke being that the workmen are used to taking orders from Bottom, and Starveling so understands Bottom's rhetoric)
186 (singular of dice: one die, two dice)
187 die with one pip/point facing up, indicating the number 1
188 ace man = unlucky/misfortunate man
189 medical man, doctor
190 show himself to be
191 does it come about/happen (verb)
192 suffering

Hippolyta Methinks she should not use[193] a long one for such a
Pyramus. I hope she will be brief.

Demetrius A mote[194] will turn the balance,[195] which Pyramus,   310
which Thisbe, is the better – he for a man, God warrant[196]
us, she for a woman, God bless us.

Lysander She hath spied him already with those sweet eyes.

Demetrius And thus she means,[197] videlicet[198] –

Flute   Asleep, my love?   315
What, dead, my dove?
O Pyramus, arise,
Speak, speak. Quite dumb?
Dead, dead? A tomb
Must cover thy sweet eyes.   320
These lily lips,
This cherry nose,
These yellow cowslip cheeks,[199]
Are gone, are gone.
Lovers, make moan.   325
His eyes were green as leeks.[200]
O Sisters Three,[201]
Come, come to me,

193 observe, perform, engage in
194 particle of dust
195 turn the balance = make one of the scale's two pans dip, registering a
    weight differential
196 protect
197 complains, laments, mourns
198 in other words, namely (language used in legal documents, when
    introducing a formal protest)
199 (describing eyes and lips of a more feminine sort, nose and cheeks of an
    unwell kind)
200 (a kind of onion, and very green)
201 (that is, the Fates)

With hands as pale as milk.
330   Lay them[202] in gore,
Since you have shore[203]
With shears his thread of silk.[204]
Tongue, not a word.
Come trusty sword,
335   Come blade, my breast imbrue.[205]

SHE STABS HERSELF

And farewell friends.
Thus Thisbe ends.
Adieu, adieu, adieu.

SHE DIES

Theseus   Moonshine and Lion are left to bury the dead.
340 *Demetrius*   Ay, and Wall too.
Bottom   No, I assure you. The wall is down, that parted their
fathers. Will it please you to see the epilogue, or to hear[206] a
Bergomask[207] dance between two of our company?
Theseus   No epilogue, I pray you. For your play needs no
345   excuse.[208] Never excuse.[209] For when the players are all
dead, there needs none to be blamed. Marry, if he that writ it

202 lay them = place your (the Fates') hands
203 cut ("shorn")
204 thread of silk = silklike thread of life
205 pierce, thrust, plunge
206 (*hear* a dance?)
207 rustic/clownish dance of Italian origin
208 apology (dramatic epilogues were frequently apologetic/placating in
    tone)(ekSKYUWS)
209 ekSKYUWZ (verb)

had played Pyramus, and hanged himself in Thisbe's garter,[210]
it would have been a fine tragedy. And so it is, truly, and very
notably discharged. But come, your Bergomask. Let your
epilogue alone.[211]   350

A DANCE. EXEUNT PLAYERS

The iron tongue[212] of midnight hath told[213] twelve.
Lovers, to bed, 'tis almost fairy time.
I fear we shall outsleep the coming morn,
As much as we this night have overwatched.[214]
This palpable gross[215] play hath well beguiled   355
The heavy gait[216] of night. Sweet friends, to bed.
A fortnight hold we[217] this solemnity,
In nightly revels and new jollity.

ALL LEAVE THE STAGE

ENTER PUCK

Puck   Now the hungry lion roars.
         And the wolf behowls the moon,   360
         Whilst the heavy[218] ploughman snores,
         All with weary task fordone.[219]

210 band worn around the leg, to hold up a stocking
211 let your epilogue alone = abstain from your epilogue
212 iron tongue = clapper of a bell, sounding out midnight
213 counted out
214 exhaust/weary oneself by staying awake too long
215 palpable gross = obviously/plainly coarse/rough/clumsy
216 heavy gait = solemn/ponderous/slow walk
217 hold we = we will keep/sustain
218 hard-working
219 exhausted

Now the wasted brands[220] do glow,

Whilst the screech owl, screeching loud,

365   Puts the wretch that lies in woe[221]

In remembrance of[222] a shroud.[223]

Now it is the time of night

That the graves, all gaping[224] wide,[225]

Every one lets forth his sprite,

370   In the churchway paths[226] to glide.[227]

And we fairies, that do run

By[228] the triple[229] Hecate's[230] team,[231]

From the presence of the sun,

Following darkness like a dream,

375   Now are frolic.[232] Not a mouse

Shall disturb this hallowed[233] house.

I am sent with broom before,[234]

---

220 wasted brands = fire-diminished pieces of wood, burning on the hearth
221 grief, misery, misfortune
222 in remembrance of = to thinking about
223 winding sheet, the cloth wrapped around a corpse (IN reMEMbrance OF a SHROUD)
224 opening
225 THAT the GRAVES all GAPing WIDE
226 churchway paths = public roads leading to a church (churchyards were burial grounds)
227 move smoothly / easily
228 beside, near
229 (1) Hecate/Proserpina in Hades, (2) Diana on earth, (3) Luna/Phoebe/Cynthia in the sky
230 HECates
231 draught animals, usually horses, harnessed together
232 mirthful, joyous
233 sanctified, consecrated, blessed
234 in advance

To sweep the dust behind[235] the door.

Oberon   Through the house give[237] glimmering light,
           By[238] the dead and drowsy fire,   380
           Every elf and fairy sprite
           Hop as light as bird from brier,
           And this ditty[239] after me,
           Sing and dance it trippingly.[240]

Titania   First rehearse[241] your song by rote,[242]   385
           To each word a warbling[243] note.
           Hand in hand, with fairy grace,
           Will we sing, and bless this place.

Oberon   Now, until the break of day,
           Through this house each fairy stray.[244]   390
           To the best bride-bed will we,
           Which by us shall blessèd be.
           And the issue,[245] there create,[246]

235 from behind (Puck/Robin Goodfellow was supposed to help with
    household chores)
236 (probably holding or wearing longish candles/tapers)
237 supply, furnish, spread, distribute
238 near, beside
239 song, ballad
240 light-footed, nimbly
241 recite, perform
242 by memory? all together?
243 melodic
244 roam, wander
245 offspring, descendants ("children")
246 created, conceived

Ever shall be fortunate.[247]

395 So shall all the couples three
Ever true in loving be.
And the blots[248] of Nature's hand
Shall not in their issue stand.[249]
Never mole, hare lip, nor scar,[250]
400 Nor mark prodigious,[251] such as are
Despisèd in nativity,
Shall upon their children be.
With[252] this field-dew consecrate,[253]
Every fairy take his gait,
405 And each several[254] chamber bless,[255]
Through this palace, with sweet peace,
And the owner of it blest[256]
Ever shall in safety rest.
Trip away, make no stay,
410 Meet me all by break of day.

EXEUNT OBERON, TITANIA, AND TRAIN

Puck   If we shadows have offended,
Think but this, and all is mended:

247 prosperous, favored by fortune (FORtyunATE)
248 stains, disfigurements
249 be, exist, be present
250 NEver MOLE hair LIP nor SCAR
251 ominous, portentous
252 (which the fairies are carrying)
253 field-dew consecrate (adjective) = consecrated/sanctified dew from fields/
    meadows
254 separate
255 AND each SEVral CHAMber BLESS
256 owner of it blest = the blessed possessor of each such room

That you have but[257] slumbered here,
While these visions did appear.
And this weak and idle theme,[258]   415
No more yielding but[259] a dream,
Gentles, do not reprehend.[260]
If you pardon, we will mend.[261]
And as I am an honest Puck,
If we have unearnèd[262] luck,   420
Now to 'scape the serpent's tongue,[263]
We will make amends[264] ere long –
Else the Puck a liar call.
So good night unto you all.
Give me your hands, if we be friends,[265]   425
And Robin shall restore[266] amends.

FINIS[267]

257 only, just
258 subject
259 yielding but – fertile/productive than
260 censure, find fault with
261 (1) correct, remove defects (from the play), (2) improve (ourselves/our
    acting/performance)
262 unmerited, undeserved
263 hissing (the sound made by serpents and by disapproving audiences)
264 reparation, satisfaction
265 clap your hands for us, if you like what we have done
266 give back
267 the end

AN ESSAY BY HAROLD BLOOM

In the midst of the winter of 1595–96, Shakespeare visualized an ideal summer, and he composed *A Midsummer Night's Dream,* probably on commission for a noble marriage, where first it was played. He had written *Richard II* and *Romeo and Juliet* during 1595; just ahead would come *The Merchant of Venice* and Fallstaff's advent in *Henry IV, Part One.* Nothing by Shakespeare before *A Midsummer Night's Dream* is its equal, and in some respects nothing by him afterward surpasses it. It is his first undoubted masterwork, without flaw, and one of his dozen or so plays of overwhelming originality and power. Unfortunately, every production of it that I have been able to attend has been a brutal disaster, with the exception of Peter Hall's motion picture of 1968, happily available on videotape. Only *The Tempest* is as much distorted in recent stagings as *A Midsummer Night's Dream* has been and is likely to go on being. The worst I recall are Peter Brook's (1970) and Alvin Epstein's (a Yale hilarity of 1975), but I cannot be the only lover of the play who rejects the prevailing notion that sexual violence and bestiality are at the center of this humane and wise drama.

Sexual politics is too much in fashion for me just to shudder and pass by; *A Midsummer Night's Dream* will reassert itself, at a better time than this, but I have much to say on behalf of Bottom, Shakespeare's most engaging character before Falstaff. Bottom, as the play's text comically makes clear, has considerably less sexual interest in Titania than she does in him, or than many recent critics and directors have in her. Shakespeare, here and elsewhere, is bawdy but not prurient; Bottom is amiably innocent, and not very bawdy. Sex-and-violence exalters really should look elsewhere; *Titus Andronicus* would be a fine start. If Shakespeare had desired to write an orgiastic ritual, with Bottom as "this Bacchic ass of Saturnalia and carnival" (Jan Kott), we would have a different comedy. What we do have is a gentle, mild, good-natured Bottom, who is rather more inclined to the company of the elves—Peaseblossom, Cobweb, Moth, and Mustardseed—than to the madly infatuated Titania. In an age of critical and theatrical absurdity, I may yet live to be told that Bottom's interest in the little folk represents a potential for child abuse, which would be no sillier than the ongoing accounts of *A Midsummer Night's Dream*.

It is a curious link between *The Tempest, Love's Labour's Lost,* and *A Midsummer Night's Dream* that these are the three plays, out of thirty-nine, where Shakespeare does not follow a primary source. Even *The Merry Wives of Windsor,* which has no definite source, takes a clear starting point from Ovid. *The Tempest* is essentially plotless, and almost nothing happens in *Love's Labour's Lost,* but Shakespeare uniquely took pains to work out a fairly elaborate and outrageous plot for *A Midsummer Night's Dream.* Inventing plot was not a Shakespearean gift; it was the one dramatic talent that nature had denied him. I think he prided himself of creating and intertwining the four different worlds of character in the *Dream*. Theseus and Hippolyta belong to ancient myth and legend. The lovers—Hermia, Helena, Lysander, and Deme-trius—are of no definite time or place, since all young people in love notoriously dwell in a common element. The fairies—Tita-nia, Oberon, Puck, and Bottom's four chums—emerge from lit-erary folklore and its magic. And finally, the "mechanicals" are English rustic artisans—the sublime Bottom, Peter Quince, Flute, Snout, Snug, and Starveling—and so come out of Shakespeare's own countryside, where he grew up.

This mélange is so diverse that a defense of it becomes the hid-den reference in the wonderfully absurd exchanges between The-seus and Hippolyta concerning the music of the hounds in act 4, scene 1, lines 103–27, which I will consider in some detail later. "So musical a discord, such sweet thunder" has been widely and correctly taken as this play's description of itself. G. K. Chester-ton, who sometimes thought the *Dream* the greatest of all Shake-speare's plays, found its "supreme literary merit" to be "a merit of design."

As an epithalamium, the *Dream* ends with three weddings, and the reconciliation of Oberon and Titania. But we might not know that all this was an extended and elaborate marriage song if the scholars did not tell us, and from the title on we do know that it is (at least in part) a dream. Whose dream? One answer is: Bot-tom's dream or his weaving, because he *is* the protagonist (and the greatest glory) of the play. Puck's epilogue, however, calls it the audience's dream, and we do not know precisely how to receive Puck's apologia. Bottom is universal enough (like James Joyce's Poldy Bloom or Earwicker) to weave a common dream for all of us, except insofar as we are Pucks rather than Bottoms. How are we meant to understand the play's title? C. L. Barber pointed out Dr. Johnson's error in believing that "the rite of May" must take place on May Day, since the young went Maying when the impulse moved them. We are neither at May Day nor at Midsummer Eve, and so the title probably should be read as *any* night at all in midsummer. There is a casual, throwaway gesture in the title: this could be anyone's dream or any night in midsummer, when the world is largest.

Bottom is Shakespeare's Everyman, a true original, a clown rather than a fool or jester. He is a wise clown, though he smilingly denies his palpable wisdom, as if his innocent vanity did not extend to such pretension. One delights in Falstaff (unless one is an academic moralist), but one loves Bottom, though necessarily he is the lesser figure of the two. No one in Shakespeare, not even Hamlet or Rosalind, Iago or Edmund, is more intelligent than Falstaff. Bottom is as shrewd as he is kind, but he is not a wit, and Falstaff is Monarch of Wit. Every exigency finds Bottom round and ready: his response is always admirable. The Puck-induced metamorphosis is a mere externality: the inner Bottom is unfazed and immutable. Shakespeare foregrounds Bottom by showing us that he is the favorite of his fellow mechanicals: they acclaim him as "bully Bottom," and we learn to agree with them.

Like Dogberry after him, Bottom is an ancester of Richard Sheridan's Mrs. Malaprop, and uses certain words without knowing what they signify. Though he is thus sometimes inaccurate at the circumference, he is always sound at the core, which is what Bottom the Weaver's name means, the center of the skein upon which the weaver's wool is wound. There are folkloric magical associations attendant upon weaving, and Puck's choice of Bottom for enchantment is therefore not as arbitrary as first it seems. Whether or not Bottom (very briefly) becomes the carnal lover of the Fairy Queen Shakespeare leaves ambiguous or elliptical, probably because it is unimportant compared with Bottom's uniqueness in the *Dream:* he alone sees and converses with the fairy folk. The childlike fourfold of Peaseblossom, Moth, Cobweb, and Mustardseed are as charmed by Bottom as he is by them. They recognize themselves in the amiable weaver, and he beholds much that is already his own in them. "On the loftiest of the world's thrones we still are sitting on our own Bottom," Montaigne taught Shakespeare and the rest of us in his greatest essay, "Of Experience." Bottom the natural man is also the transcendental Bottom, who is just as happily at home with Cobweb and Peaseblossom as he is with Snug and Peter Quince. For him there is no musical discord or confusion in the overlapping realms of the *Dream*. It is absurd to condescend to Bottom: he is at once a sublime clown and a great visionary.

There is no darkness in Bottom, even when he is caught up in an enchanted condition. Puck, his antithesis, is an ambivalent figure, a mischief maker at best, and something weirder also, though the play (and Oberon) confine him to harmlessness, and indeed bring benignity out of his antics. Puck's alternate name in both the play and in popular lore is Robin Goodfellow, more a prankster than a wicked sprite, though to call him "Goodfellow" suggests a need to placate him. The word *puck* or *pook* originally meant a demon out for mischief or a wicked man, and Robin Goodfellow was once a popular name for the Devil. Yet throughout the *Dream* he plays Ariel to Oberon's Prospero, and so is under firmly benign control. At the end of the play, Bottom is restored to his external guise, the lovers pair off sensibly, and Oberon and Titania resume their union. "But we are spirits of another sort," Oberon remarks, and even Puck is therefore benevolent in the *Dream*.

The Puck–Bottom contrast helps define the world of the *Dream*. Bottom, the best sort of natural man, is subject to the pranks of Puck, helpless to avoid them, and unable to escape their influence without Oberon's order of release: though the *Dream* is a romantic comedy, and not an allegory, part of its power is to suggest that Bottom and Puck are invariable components of the human. One of the etymological meanings of "bottom" is the ground or the earth, and perhaps people can be divided into the earthy and the puckish, and are so divided within themselves. And yet Bottom is human, and Puck is not; since he has no human feelings, Puck has no precise human meaning.

Bottom is an early Shakespearean instance of how meaning gets started, rather than merely repeated: as in the greater Falstaff, Shakespearean meaning comes from excess, overflow, florabundance. Bottom's consciousness, unlike Falstaff's and Hamlet's, is not infinite; we learn its circumferences, and some of them are silly. But Bottom is heroically sound in the goodness of his heart, his bravery, his ability to remain himself in any circumstance, his refusal to panic or even be startled. Like Launce and the Bastard Faulconbridge, Bottom is a triumphant early instance of Shakespeare's invention of the human. All of them are on the road to Falstaff, who will surpass them even in their exuberance of being, and vastly is beyond them as a source for meaning. Falstaff, the ultimate anarchist, is as dangerous as he is fascinating, both life-enhancing and potentially destructive. Bottom is a superb comic, and a very good man, as benign as any in Shakespeare.

Doubtless Shakespeare remembered that in Edmund Spenser's *Faerie Queene* Oberon was the benevolent father of Gloriana, who in the allegory of Spenser's great epic represented Queen

Elizabeth herself. Scholars believe it likely that Elizabeth was present at the initial performance of the *Dream,* where necessarily she would have been the Guest of Honor at the wedding. *A Midsummer Night's Dream,* like *Love's Labour's Lost, The Tempest,* and *Henry VIII,* abounds in pageantry. This aspect of the *Dream* is wonderfully analyzed in C. L. Barber's *Shakespeare's Festive Comedy,* and has little to do with my prime emphasis on the Shakespearean invention of character and personality. As an aristocratic entertainment, the *Dream* bestows relatively little of its energies upon making Theseus and Hippolyta, Oberon and Titania, and the four young lovers lost in the woods into idiosyncratic and distinct personages. Bottom and the uncanny Puck are protagonists, and are portrayed in detail. Everyone else—even the other colorful Mechanicals—are subdued to the emblematic quality that pageantry tends to require. Still, Shakespeare seems to have looked beyond the play's initial occasion to its other function as a work for the public stage, and there are small, sometimes very subtle touches of characterization that transcend the function of an aristocratic epithalamium. Hermia has considerably more personality than Helena, while Lysander and Demetrius are interchangeable, a Shakespearean irony that suggests the arbitrariness of young love, from the perspective of everyone except the lover. But then all love is ironical in the *Dream:* Hippolyta, though apparently resigned, is a captive bride, a partly tamed Amazon, while Oberon and Titania are so accustomed to mutual sexual betrayal that their actual rift has nothing to do with passion but concerns the protocol of just who has charge of a changeling human child, a little boy currently under Titania's care. Though the greatness of the *Dream* begins and ends in Bottom, who makes his first appearance in the play's second scene, and in Puck, who begins act

2, we are not transported by the sublime language unique to this
drama until Oberon and Titania first confront each other:

Oberon Ill met by moonlight, proud Titania.
Titania What, jealous Oberon? Fairies, skip hence.
   I have forsworn his bed and company.
Oberon Tarry, rash wanton. Am not I thy lord?
Titania Then I must be thy lady. But I know
   When thou hast stol'n away from fairy land,
   And in the shape of Corin sat all day
   Playing on pipes of corn and versing love
   To amorous Phillida. Why art thou here,
   Come from the farthest step of India,
   But that, forsooth, the bouncing Amazon,
   Your buskined mistress and your warrior love,
   To Theseus must be wedded, and you come
   To give their bed joy and prosperity.
Oberon How canst thou thus for shame, Titania,
   Glance at my credit with Hippolyta,
   Knowing I know thy love to Theseus?
   Didst thou not lead him through the glimmering night
   From Perigenia, whom he ravishèd,
   And make him with fair Aegle break his faith
   With Ariadne and Antiopa?

                           [2.1.60–80]

In Plutarch's *Life of Theseus,* read by Shakespeare in Sir Thomas
North's version, Theseus is credited with many "ravishments,"
cheerfully itemized here by Oberon, who assigns Titania the role
of bawd, guiding the Athenian hero to his conquests, herself
doubtless included. Though Titania will retort that "These are

the forgeries of jealousy," they are just as persuasive as her visions of Oberon "versing love / To amorous Phillida," and enjoying "the bouncing Amazon," Hippolyta. The Theseus of the *Dream* appears to have retired from his womanizings into rational respectability, with its attendant moral obtuseness. Hippolyta, though championed as a victim by feminist critics, shows little aversion to being wooed by the sword and seems content to dwindle into Athenian domesticity after her exploits with Oberon, though she retains a vision all her own, as will be seen. What Titania magnificently goes on to tell us is that discord between herself and Oberon is a disaster for both the natural and the human realm:

Titania These are the forgeries of jealousy.
    And never, since the middle summer's spring,
    Met we on hill, in dale, forest or mead,
    By pavèd fountain or by rushy brook,
    Or in the beachèd margent of the sea,
    To dance our ringlets to the whistling wind,
    But with thy brawls thou hast disturbed our sport.
    Therefore the winds, piping to us in vain,
    As in revenge have sucked up from the sea
    Contagious fogs which, falling in the land,
    Hath every pelting river made so proud
    That they have overborne their continents.
    The ox hath therefore stretched his yoke in vain,
    The ploughman lost his sweat, and the green corn
    Hath rotted ere his youth attained a beard;
    The fold stands empty in the drownèd field,
    And crows are fatted with the murrion flock.
    The nine men's morris is filled up with mud,

And the quaint mazes in the wanton green
For lack of tread are undistinguishable.
The human mortals want their winter cheer.
No night is now with hymn or carol blest.
Therefore the moon, the governess of floods,
Pale in her anger, washes all the air
That rheumatic diseases do abound.
And thorough this distemperature we see
The seasons alter. Hoary-headed frosts
Fall in the fresh lap of the crimson rose;
And on old Hiems' thin and icy crown
An odorous chaplet of sweet summer buds
Is, as in mockery, set. The spring, the summer,
The childing autumn, angry winter, change
Their wonted liveries. And the mazèd world,
By their increase, now knows not which is which.
And this same progeny of evils comes
From our debate, from our dissension.
We are their parents and original.

[2.1.81–117]

No previous poetry by Shakespeare achieved this extraordinary quality; he finds here one of his many authentic voices, the paean of natural lament. Power in the *Dream* is magical rather than political; Theseus is ignorant when he assigns power to the paternal, or to masculine sexuality. Our contemporary heirs of the materialist metaphysics of Iago, Thersites, and Edmund see Oberon as only another assertion of masculine authority, but they need to ponder Titania's lamentation. Oberon is superior in trickery, since he controls Puck, and he will win Titania back to what he considers his kind of amity. But is that a reassertion of male dominance, or of something much subtler? The issue between the fairy queen and king is a custody dispute: "I do but beg a little changeling boy / To be my henchman"—that is, Oberon's page of honor in his court. Rather than the unbounded prurience that many critics insist upon, I see nothing but an innocent assertion of sovereignty in Oberon's whim, or in Titania's poignant and beautiful refusal to yield up the child:

> Set your heart at rest:
> The fairy land buys not the child of me.
> His mother was a votress of my order,
> And in the spicèd Indian air, by night,
> Full often hath she gossiped by my side,
> And sat with me on Neptune's yellow sands,
> Marking th'embarked traders on the flood.
> When we have laughed to see the sails conceive
> And grow big-bellied with the wanton wind,
> Which she, with pretty and with swimming gait
> Following – her womb then rich with my young squire –
> Would imitate, and sail upon the land
> To fetch me trifles, and return again
> As from a voyage, rich with merchandise.
> But she, being mortal, of that boy did die,
> And for her sake do I rear up her boy,
> And for her sake I will not part with him.

> [2.1.121–137]

Ruth Nevo accurately observes that Titania has so assimilated her votaries to herself that the changeling child has become her own, in a relationship that firmly excludes Oberon. To make the

boy his henchman would be an assertion of adoption, like Prospero's initial stance toward Caliban, and Oberon will utilize Puck
to achieve this object. But why should Oberon, who is not jealous
of Theseus, and is willing to be cuckolded by Titania's enchantment, feel so fiercely in regard to the changeling's custody?
Shakespeare will not tell us, and so we must interpret this ellipsis
for ourselves.

One clear implication is that Oberon and Titania have no male
child of their own; Oberon being immortal need not worry
about an heir, but evidently he has paternal aspirations that his
henchman Puck cannot satisfy. It may also be relevant that the
changeling boy's father was an Indian king, and that tradition
traces Oberon's royal lineage to an Indian emperor. What matters
most appears to be Titania's refusal to allow Oberon any share in
her adoption of the child. Perhaps David Wiles is correct in argu-
ing that Oberon desires to parallel the pattern of Elizabethan aristocratic marriages, where the procreation of a male heir was the
highest object, though Elizabeth herself as Virgin Queen undoes
the tradition, and Elizabeth is the ultimate patroness of the *Dream*.

I think the quarrel between Titania and Oberon is subtler, and
turns on the question of the links between mortals and immortals
in the play. Theseus' and Hippolyta's amours with the fairies are
safely in the past, and Oberon and Titania, however estranged
from each other, have arrived in the wood near Athens to bless the
wedding of their former lovers. Bottom, one of the least likely of
mortals, will sojourn briefly among the fairies, but his metamorphosis, when it comes, is merely outward. The Indian child is a
true changeling; he will live out his life among the immortals.
That is anything but irrelevant to Oberon: he and his subjects
have their mysteries, jealously guarded from mortals. To exclude

Oberon from the child's company is therefore not just a challenge to male authority; it is a wrong done to Oberon, and one that he must reverse and subsume in the name of the legitimacy in leadership that he shares with Titania. As Oberon says, it is an "injury."

To torment Titania away from her resolution, Oberon invokes what becomes the most beautiful of Shakespeare's visions in the play:

Oberon   Thou rememb'rest
   Since once I sat upon a promontory,
   And heard a mermaid on a dolphin's back
   Uttering such dulcet and harmonious breath
   That the rude sea grew civil at her song
   And certain stars shot madly from their spheres
   To hear the sea maid's music?
Puck   I remember.
Oberon That very time I saw, but thou couldst not,
   Flying between the cold moon and the earth,
   Cupid all armed. A certain aim he took
   At a fair vestal thronèd by the west,
   And loosed his love-shaft smartly from his bow
   As it should pierce a hundred thousand hearts.
   But I might see young Cupid's fiery shaft
   Quenched in the chaste beams of the watery moon,
   And the imperial votress passèd on,
   In maiden meditation, fancy free.
   Yet marked I where the bolt of Cupid fell.
   It fell upon a little western flower,
   Before milk white, now purple with love's wound,
   And maidens call it "love-in-idleness."

Fetch me that flower. The herb I show'd thee once.
The juice of it on sleeping eyelids laid
Will make or man or woman madly dote
Upon the next live creature that it sees.
Fetch me this herb, and be thou here again
Ere the leviathan can swim a league.

Puck   I'll put a girdle round about the earth
In forty minutes.

Oberon   Having once this juice,
I'll watch Titania when she is asleep,
And drop the liquor of it in her eyes.
The next thing then she, waking, looks upon,
Be it on lion, bear, or wolf, or bull,
On meddling monkey, or on busy ape,
She shall pursue it with the soul of love.
And ere I take this charm from off her sight,
As I can take it with another herb,
I'll make her render up her page to me.

[2.1.148–185]

The flower love-in-idleness is the pansy; the "fair vestal, throned by the west" is Queen Elizabeth I, and one function of this fairy vision is to constitute Shakespeare's largest and most direct tribute to his monarch during her lifetime. She passes on, and remains fancy free; the arrow of Cupid, unable to wound the Virgin Queen, instead converts the pansy into a universal love charm. It is as though Elizabeth's choice of chastity opens up a cosmos of erotic possibilities for others, but at the high cost of accident and arbitrariness replacing her reasoned choice. Love at first sight, exalted in *Romeo and Juliet,* is pictured here as calamity.

The ironic possibilities of the love elixir are first intimated when, in one of the play's most exquisite passages, Oberon plots the ensnarement of Titania:

> I know a bank where the wild thyme blows,
> Where oxlips and the nodding violet grows,
> Quite over-canopied with luscious woodbine,
> With sweet musk-roses and with eglantine.
> There sleeps Titania sometime of the night,
> Lulled in these flowers with dances and delight.
> And there the snake throws her enameled skin,
> Weed wide enough to wrap a fairy in.
> And with the juice of this I'll streak her eyes,
> And make her full of hateful fantasies.

> [2.1.249–258]

The contrast between those first six lines and the four that come after grants us an aesthetic *frisson;* the transition is from John Keats and Alfred, Lord Tennyson to Robert Browning and the early T. S. Eliot, as Oberon modulates from sensuous naturalism to grotesque gusto. Shakespeare thus prepares the way for the play's great turning point in act 3, scene 1, where Puck transforms Bottom, and Titania wakens with the great outcry, "What angel wakes me from my flow'ry bed?" The angel is the imperturbable Bottom, who is sublimely undismayed that his amiable countenance has metamorphosed into an ass head.

This wonderfully comic scene deserves pondering: Who among us could sustain so weird a calamity with so equable a spirit? One feels that Bottom could have undergone the fate of Franz Kafka's Gregor Samsa with only moderate chagrin. He enters almost on cue, chanting, "If I were fair, Thisbe, I were only thine," scattering his fellows. Presumably discouraged at his inability to frighten Bottom, the frustrated Puck chases after the Mechanicals, taking on many fearsome guises. Our bully Bottom responds to Peter Quince's "Bless thee, Bottom, bless thee! Thou art translated," by cheerfully singing a ditty hinting at cuckoldry, thus preparing us for a comic dialogue that even Shakespeare was never to surpass:

Titania I pray thee, gentle mortal, sing again.
   Mine ear is much enamored of thy note.
   So is mine eye enthralled to thy shape,
   And thy fair virtue's force perforce doth move me
   On the first view to say, to swear, I love thee.
Bottom Methinks, mistress, you should have little reason for that.
   And yet, to say the truth, reason and love keep little company
   together nowadays. The more the pity, that some honest
   neighbors will not make them friends. Nay, I can gleek upon
   occasion.
Titania Thou art as wise as thou art beautiful.
Bottom Not so, neither. But if I had wit enough to get out of
   this wood, I have enough to serve mine own turn.
Titania Out of this wood do not desire to go.
   Thou shalt remain here, whether thou wilt or no.

                      [3.1.132–146]

Even C. L. Barber somewhat underestimates Bottom, when he says that Titania and Bottom are "fancy against fact," since "enchantment against Truth" is more accurate. Bottom is unfailingly courteous, courageous, kind, and sweet-tempered, and he humors the beautiful queen whom he clearly knows to be quite mad. The ironies here are fully in Bottom's control, and are kept gentle by his tact. Nothing else in the *Dream* is as pithy an account of its erotic confusions: "reason and love keep little company together nowadays." Bottom too can "gleek" (jest) upon occasion, which is the only other possibility, should poor Titania prove to be sane. Neither wise nor beautiful, Bottom sensibly wishes to get out of the wood, but he does not seem particularly alarmed when Titania tells him he is a prisoner. Her proud assertion of rank and self is hilarious in its absurd confidence that she can purge Bottom's "mortal grossness" and transform him into another "airy spirit," as though he could be another changeling like the Indian boy:

Titania I am a spirit of no common rate.
  The summer, still, doth tend upon my state,
  And I do love thee. Therefore, go with me.
  I'll give thee fairies to attend on thee.
  And they shall fetch thee jewels from the deep,
  And sing while thou on pressèd flowers dost sleep.
  And I will purge thy mortal grossness so,
  That thou shalt like an airy spirit go.
  Peaseblossom! Cobweb! Moth! and Mustardseed!

                                        [3.1.136– 144]

Bottom, amiable enough to the infatuated Titania, is truly charmed by the four elves, and they by Bottom, who would be one of them even without benefit of Puckish translation:

Peaseblossom Ready.
Cobweb   And I.
Moth   And I.
Mustardseed   And I.
All   Where shall we go?
Titania   Be kind and courteous to this gentleman,

Hop in his walks and gambol in his eyes,
Feed him with apricocks and dewberries,
With purple grapes, green figs, and mulberries,
The honey bags steal from the humble bees,
And for night-tapers crop their waxen thighs,
And light them at the fiery glow worm's eyes,
To have my love to bed and to arise,
And pluck the wings from painted butterflies
To fan the moonbeams from his sleeping eyes.
Nod to him, elves, and do him courtesies.

Peaseblossom Hail, mortal!

Cobweb   Hail!

Moth   Hail!

Mustardseed   Hail!

Bottom   I cry your worships mercy, heartily. I beseech your worship's name?

Cobweb   Cobweb.

Bottom   I shall desire you of more acquaintance, good Master Cobweb. If I cut my finger, I shall make bold with you. Your name, honest gentleman?

Peaseblossom Peaseblossom.

Bottom   I pray you, commend me to Mistress Squash, your mother, and to Master Peascod, your father. Good Master Peaseblossom, I shall desire you of more acquaintance, too. Your name, I beseech you, sir?

Mustardseed   Mustardseed.

Bottom   Good Master Mustardseed, I know your patience well. That same cowardly giant-like ox-beef hath devoured many a gentleman of your house. I promise you your kindred

hath made my eyes water, ere now. I desire you of more
acquaintance, good Master Mustardseed.

[3.1.145–175]

Though Titania will follow this colloquy of innocents by or-
dering the elves to lead Bottom to her bower, it remains ambiguous exactly what transpires there admist the nodding violet, luscious woodbine, and sweet musk roses. If you are not Jan Kott or
Peter Brook, does it matter? Does one remember the play for "orgiastic bestiality" or for Peaseblossom, Cobweb, Moth, and Mustardseed? Undoubtedly played by children then, as they are now,
these elves are adept at stealing from honeybees and butterflies, a
precarious art emblematic of the entire *Dream*. Bottom's grave
courtesy to them and their cheerful attentiveness to help help es-
tablish an affinity that suggests what is profoundly childlike (not
childish, not bestial) about Bottom. The problem with reacting to
resenters is that I sometimes hear the voice of my late mentor,
Frederick A. Pottle, of Yale, admonishing me: "Mr. Bloom, stop
beating dead woodchucks!" I will do so, and am content to cite
William Empson on Kott: "I take my stand beside the other old
buffers here. Kott is ridiculously indifferent to the Letter of the
play and labors to befoul its spirit."

Fairies in general (Puck in particular) are likely to miss one tar-
get and hit another. Instructed by Oberon to divert Demetrius'
passion from Hermia to Helena, Puck errs and transforms Lysander into Helena's pursuer. When Puck gets it right at second try,
the foursome become more absurd than ever, with Helena, believing herself mocked, fleeing both suitors, while Hermia lan-
guishes in a state of amazement. Act 3 concludes with all four ex-

hausted lovers being put to sleep by Puck, who carefully re-arranges Lysander's affections to their original object, Hermia, while keeping Demetrius enthralled by Helena. This raises the happy irony that the play will never resolve: Does it make any dif-ference at all who marries whom? Shakespeare's pragmatic an-swer is: Not much, whether in this comedy or another, since all marriages seem in Shakespeare to be headed for unhappiness. Shakespeare seems always to hold what I call the "black box" the-ory of object choice. The airliner goes down, and we seek out the black box to learn the cause of the catastrophe, but our black boxes are unfindable, and our marital disasters are as arbitrary as our successes. Perhaps this should be called "Puck's Law": Who can say whether Demetrius-Helena or Lysander-Hermia will prove the better match? Act 3 of the *Dream* brushes aside any such question, ending as it does with Puck singing:

Jack shall have Jill,
Nought shall go ill.

[3.2.461–462]

Everyone should collect favorite acts in Shakespeare; one of mine would be act 4 of the *Dream,* where wonder crowds wonder and eloquence overflows, as Shakespeare manifests his creative exu-berance without pause. The orgiastic reading is prophetically dis-missed by the first scene, where Titania sits the amiable Bottom down upon a flowery bed, caresses his cheeks, sticks musk roses in his head, and kisses his ears. This scarcely arouses Bottom to lust:

Bottom　　　Where's Peaseblossom?
Peaseblossom　Ready.

Bottom   Scratch my head, Peaseblossom. Where's
Mounsieur Cobweb?

Cobweb   Ready.

Bottom   Mounsieur Cobweb, good mounsieur, get you
your weapons in your hand, and kill me a red-hipped
humblebee on the top of a thistle. And good mounsieur,
bring me the honey bag. Do not fret yourself too much in the
action, mounsieur. And good mounsieur, have a care the
honey bag break not. I would be loath to have you
overflowen with a honey bag, signior. Where's Mounsieur
Mustardseed?

Mustardseed Ready.

Bottom   Give me your neaf, Mounsieur Mustardseed. Pray
you, leave your courtesy, good mounsieur.

Mustardseed What's your will?

Bottom   Nothing, good mounsieur, but to help Cavalery
Cobweb to scratch. I must to the barber's, mounsieur, for
methinks I am marvelous hairy about the face, and I am such
a tender ass, if my hair do but tickle me, I must scratch.

Titania   What, wilt thou hear some music, my sweet love?

Bottom   I have a reasonable good ear in music. Let's have the
tongs and the bones.

Titania   Or say, sweet love, what thou desirest to eat.

Bottom   Truly, a peck of provender. I could munch your
good dry oats. Methinks I have a great desire to a bottle of
hay. Good hay, sweet hay, hath no fellow.

[4.1.5–32]

What hath Puck wrought: for Titania, a considerable indig-
nity, no doubt, but for Bottom a friendship with four elves. Since

Bottom is getting drowsy, we can understand his mixing up Cobweb with Peaseblossom, but he is otherwise much himself, even if his eating habits perforce are altered. He falls asleep, entwined with the rapt Titania, in a charmingly innocent embrace. Oberon informs us that, since she has surrendered the changeling boy to him, all is forgiven so that Puck can cure her enchantment, and in passing, Bottom's, though the weaver resolutely goes on sleeping. Shakespeare's touch here is astonishingly light; metamorphoses are represented by the dance of reconciliation that restores the marriage of Oberon and Titania:

> Come, my queen, take hands with me,
> And rock the ground whereon these sleepers be.

> [4.1.84–85]

The four lovers and Bottom stay fast asleep even as Theseus, Hippolyta, and their train make a boisterous entry with a dialogue that is Shakespeare's bravura defense of his art of fusion in this play:

Theseus Go, one of you, find out the forester.
For now our observation is perform'd.
And since we have the vaward of the day,
My love shall hear the music of my hounds.
Uncouple in the western valley, let them go.
Dispatch, I say, and find the forester.

EXIT ATTENDANT

We will, fair queen, up to the mountain's top,
And mark the musical confusion
Of hounds and echo in conjunction.

Hippolyta I was with Hercules and Cadmus once,
    When in a wood of Crete they bayed the bear,
    With hounds of Sparta. Never did I hear
    Such gallant chiding, for besides the groves,
    The skies, the fountains, every region near
    Seemed all one mutual cry. I never heard
    So musical a discord, such sweet thunder.
Theseus   My hounds are bred out of the Spartan kind,
    So flewed, so sanded. And their heads are hung
    With ears that sweep away the morning dew,
    Crook-kneed, and dewlapped like Thessalian bulls –
    Slow in pursuit, but matched in mouth like bells,
    Each under each. A cry more tuneable
    Was never holla'd to, nor cheered with horn,
    In Crete, in Sparta, nor in Thessaly.
    Judge when you hear. But soft, what nymphs are these?

                                           [4.1.102–130]

The musical discord holds together four different modes of representation: Theseus and Hippolyta, from classical legend; the four young lovers, from every place and every time; Bottom and his fellow English rustics; the fairies, who in themselves are madly eclectic. Titania is Ovid's alternate name for Diana, while Oberon comes out of Celtic romance, and Puck or Robin Goodfellow is English folklore. In their delightfully insane dialogue, Theseus and Hippolyta join in celebrating the wonderful nonsense of the Spartan hounds, bred only for their baying, so that they are "slow in pursuit." Shakespeare celebrates the "sweet thunder" of his comic extravagance, which like Theseus' hounds is in no particular hurry to get anywhere, and which still has superb surprises for us. I pass over the awakening of the four lovers (Demetrius now in love with Helena) to come at the finest speech Shakespeare had yet written, Bottom's sublime reverie upon waking up:

Bottom When my cue comes, call me, and I will answer. My
next is, "Most fair Pyramus." Heigh-ho! Peter Quince? Flute,
the bellowsmender? Snout, the tinker? Starveling? God's my
life, stolen hence, and left me asleep! I have had a most rare
vision. I have had a dream, past the wit of man to say what
dream it was. Man is but an ass, if he go about to expound this
dream. Methought I was – there is no man can tell what.
Methought I was – and methought I had – but man is but a
patch'd fool, if he will offer to say what methought I had. The
eye of man hath not heard, the ear of man hath not seen,
man's hand is not able to taste, his tongue to conceive, nor his
heart to report, what my dream was. I will get Peter Quince
to write a ballad of this dream. It shall be called "Bottom's
Dream," because it hath no bottom. And I will sing it in the
latter end of a play, before the Duke. Peradventure, to make it
the more gracious, I shall sing it at her death.

[4.1.200–216]

"The Spirite searcheth . . . the botome of Goddes secretes," is the Geneva Bible's rendering of 1 Corinthians 2:9–10. Bottom's parody of 1 Corinthians 2:9 is audacious, and allows Shakespeare to anticipate William Blake's Romantic vision, with its repudiation of the Pauline split between flesh and spirit, though Bottom seems to have heard the text preached to him in the Bishops' Bible version: "The eye hath not seene, and the eare hath not heard, neyther have entered into the heart of man, the things which God hath purposed. . . ."

For Bottom, "the eye . . . hath not heard, the ear . . . hath not seen, [the] hand is not able to taste, his tongue to conceive, nor his heart to report" the truths of his bottomless dream. Like William Blake after him, Bottom suggests an apocalyptic, unfallen man, whose awakened senses fuse in a synesthetic unity. It is difficult not to find in Bottom, in this his sublimest moment, an ancestor not just of Blake's Albion but of Joyce's Earwicker, the universal dreamer of *Finnegans Wake*. Bottom's greatness—Shakespeare upon his heights—emerges most strongly in what could be called "Bottom's Vision," a mysterious triumph he is to enjoy before Theseus as audience, where the "play" cannot be the mere travesty, the play-within-the-play *Pyramus and Thisbe*:

> I will get Peter Quince to write a ballad of this dream. It shall be called "Bottom's Dream," because it hath no bottom. And I will sing it in the latter end of a play, before the Duke. Peradventure, to make it the more gracious, I shall sing it at her death.

Whose death? Since we do not know the visionary drama playing out in Bottom's consciousness, we cannot answer the question, except to say that it is neither Titania nor Thisbe. When, in the next scene, sweet bully Bottom returns joyously to his friends, he will not speak in these tones. Shakespeare, though, has not forgotten this "more gracious" aspect of Bottom, and subtly opposes it to the famous speech of Theseus that opens act 5. Hippolyta muses on the strangeness of the story told by the four young lovers, and Theseus opposes his skepticism to her wonder.

Theseus More strange than true. I never may believe
These antique fables, nor these fairy toys.

Lovers and madmen have such seething brains,
Such shaping fantasies, that apprehend
More than cool reason ever comprehends.
The lunatic, the lover, and the poet
Are of imagination all compact.
One sees more devils than vast hell can hold:
That is the madman. The lover, all as frantic,
Sees Helen's beauty in a brow of Egypt.
The poet's eye, in a fine frenzy, rolling,
Doth glance from heaven to earth, from earth to heaven;
And as imagination bodies forth
The forms of things unknown, the poet's pen
Turns them to shapes and gives to airy nothing
A local habitation, and a name.
Such tricks hath strong imagination,
That if it would but apprehend some joy,
It comprehends some bringer of that joy.
Or in the night, imagining some fear,
How easy is a bush supposed a bear?

[5.1.2–22]

Theseus himself could be called, not unkindly, "highly un-imaginative," but there are two voices here, and one perhaps is Shakespeare's own, half-distancing itself from its own art, though declining also to yield completely to the patronizing Theseus. When Shakespeare writes these lines, the lover sees Helen's beauty in a gypsy girl's brow, and yet the prophetic consciousness somewhere in Shakespeare anticipates Antony seeing Helen's beauty in Cleopatra. "Imagination," to Shakespeare's contemporaries, was "fantasy," a powerful but suspect faculty of the mind. Sir

Francis Bacon neatly stated this ambiguity: "Neither is the Imagination simply and only a messenger; but is invested with or at leastwise usurpeth no small authority in itself, besides the duty of the message."

"Usurpeth" is the key word there; the mind for Bacon is the legitimate authority, and imagination should be content to be the mind's messenger, and to assert no authority for itself. Theseus is more a Baconian than a Shakespearean, but Hippolyta breaks away from Theseus's dogmatism:

> But all the story of the night told over,
> And all their minds transfigured so together,
> More witnesseth than fancy's images,
> And grows to something of great constancy.
> But howsoever, strange and admirable.
>
> [5.1.23–27]

You could give Hippolyta's lines a rather minimal interpretation, stressing that she herself distrusts "fancy's images," but that seems to me a woeful reading. For Theseus, poetry is a furor, and the poet a trickster; Hippolyta opens to a greater resonance, to transfiguration that affects more than one mind at once. The lovers are her metaphor for the Shakespearean audience, and it is ourselves, therefore, who grow into "something of great constancy," and so are re-formed, strangely and admirably. Hippolyta's majestic gravity is an implicit rebuke to Theseus' scoffing at the poet's "fine frenzy." Critics rightly have expanded their apprehension of Shakespeare's "story of the night" beyond the *Dream,* marvelous as the play is. "No, I assure you. The wall is down, that parted their fathers" is Bottom's final resonance in the play, and transcends Theseus' patronizing understanding. "The best in this kind are but shadows," Theseus says of all plays and playing—and while we might accept this from Macbeth, we cannot accept it from the dull Duke of Athens. Puck, in the Epilogue, only seems to agree with Theseus when he chants that "we shadows" are "but a dream," since the dream is this great play itself. The poet who dreamed Bottom was about to achieve a great dream of reality, Sir John Falstaff, who would have no interest in humoring Theseus.

FURTHER READING

This is not a bibliography but a selective set of starting places.

Texts

Shakespeare, William. *A Midsummer Night's Dream, 1600.* The Malone Society Reprints, vol. 157. Oxford: Oxford University Press, 1995.
————. *A Midsommer Nights Dreame.* New Variorum Ed., ed. Horace Howard Furness. Philadelphia: Lippincott, 1895.

Language

Houston, John Porter. *The Rhetoric of Poetry in the Renaissance and Seventeenth Century.* Baton Rouge: Louisiana State University Press, 1983.
————. *Shakespearean Sentences: A Study in Style and Syntax.* Baton Rouge: Louisiana State University Press, 1988.
Kermode, Frank. *Shakespeare's Language.* New York: Farrar, Straus and Giroux, 2000.
Kökeritz, Helge. *Shakespeare's Pronunciation.* New Haven: Yale University Press, 1953.
Lanham, Richard A. *The Motives of Eloquence: Literary Rhetoric in the Renaissance.* New Haven and London: Yale University Press, 1976.
Marcus, Leah S. *Unediting the Renaissance: Shakespeare, Marlowe, Milton.* London: Routledge, 1996.

The Oxford English Dictionary: Second Edition on CD-ROM, version 3.0.
New York: Oxford University Press, 2002.

Raffel, Burton. *From Stress to Stress: An Autobiography of English Prosody.*
Hamden, Conn.: Archon Books, 1992.

Ronberg, Gert. *A Way with Words: The Language of English Renaissance
Literature.* London: Arnold, 1992.

Trousdale, Marion. *Shakespeare and the Rhetoricians.* Chapel Hill:
University of North Carolina Press, 1982.

Culture

Bindoff, S.T. *Tudor England.* Baltimore: Penguin, 1950.

Bradbrook, M. C. *Shakespeare: The Poet in His World.* New York:
Columbia University Press, 1978.

Brown, Cedric C., ed. *Patronage, Politics, and Literary Tradition in England,
1558–1658.* Detroit, Mich.: Wayne State University Press, 1993.

Buxton, John. *Elizabethan Taste.* London: Harvester, 1963.

Cowan, Alexander. *Urban Europe, 1500–1700.* New York: Oxford
University Press, 1998.

Finucci, Valeria, and Regina Schwartz, eds. *Desire in the Renaissance:
Psychoanalysis and Literature.* Princeton, N.J.: Princeton University
Press, 1994.

Fumerton, Patricia, and Simon Hunt, eds. *Renaissance Culture and the
Everyday.* Philadelphia: University of Pennsylvania Press, 1999.

Halliday, F. E. *Shakespeare in His Age.* South Brunswick, N.J.: Yoseloff,
1965.

Harrison, G. B., ed. *The Elizabethan Journals: Being a Record of Those
Things Most Talked of During the Years 1591–1597.* Abridged ed. 2 vols.
New York: Doubleday Anchor, 1965.

Harrison, William. *The Description of England: The Classic Contemporary
[1577] Account of Tudor Social Life.* Edited by Georges Edelen.
Washington, D.C.: Folger Shakespeare Library, 1968. Reprint, New
York: Dover, 1994.

Jardine, Lisa. *Reading Shakespeare Historically.* London: Routledge, 1996.
———. *Worldly Goods: A New History of the Renaissance.* London:
Macmillan, 1996.

Jeanneret, Michel. *A Feast of Words: Banquets and Table Talk in the*

Renaissance. Translated by Jeremy Whiteley and Emma Hughes. Chicago: University of Chicago Press, 1991.

Lockyer, Roger. *Tudor and Stuart Britain.* London: Longmans, 1964.

Rose, Mary Beth, ed. *Renaissance Drama as Cultural History: Essays from Renaissance Drama, 1977–1987.* Evanston, Ill.: Northwestern University Press, 1990.

Tillyard, E. M. W. *The Elizabethan World Picture.* London: Chatto and Windus, 1943. Reprint, Harmondsworth: Penguin, 1963.

Willey, Basil. *The Seventeenth Century Background: Studies in the Thought of the Age in Relation to Poetry and Religion.* New York: Columbia University Press, 1933. Reprint, New York: Doubleday, 1955.

Wilson, F. P. *The Plague in Shakespeare's London.* 2d ed. Oxford: Oxford University Press, 1963.

Wilson, John Dover. *Life in Shakespeare's England: A Book of Elizabethan Prose.* 2d ed. Cambridge: Cambridge University Press, 1913. Reprint, Harmondsworth: Penguin, 1944.

Zimmerman, Susan, and Ronald F. E. Weissman, eds. *Urban Life in the Renaissance.* Newark: University of Delaware Press, 1989.

Dramatic Development

Cohen, Walter. *Drama of a Nation: Public Theater in Renaissance England and Spain.* Ithaca, N.Y.: Cornell University Press, 1985.

Dessen, Alan C. *Shakespeare and the Late Moral Plays.* Lincoln: University of Nebraska Press, 1986.

Fraser, Russell A., and Norman Rabkin, eds. *Drama of the English Renaissance.* 2 vols. Upper Saddle River, N.J.: Prentice Hall, 1976.

Happé, Peter, ed. *Tudor Interludes.* Harmondsworth: Penguin, 1972.

Laroque, François. *Shakespeare's Festive World: Elizabethan Seasonal Entertainment and the Professional Stage.* Translated by Janet Lloyd. Cambridge: Cambridge University Press, 1991.

Norland, Howard B. *Drama in Early Tudor Britain, 1485–1558.* Lincoln: University of Nebraska Press, 1995.

Theater and Stage

Doran, Madeleine. *Endeavors of Art: A Study of Form in Elizabethan Drama.* Milwaukee: University of Wisconsin Press, 1954.

Gurr, Andrew. *Playgoing in Shakespeare's London*. Cambridge: Cambridge University Press, 1987.

————. *The Shakespearian Stage, 1574–1642*. 3d ed. Cambridge: Cambridge University Press, 1992.

Harrison, G. B. *Elizabethan Plays and Players*. Ann Arbor: University of Michigan Press, 1956.

Holmes, Martin. *Shakespeare and His Players*. New York: Scribners, 1972.

Ingram, William. *The Business of Playing: The Beginnings of the Adult Professional Theater in Elizabethan London*. Ithaca, N.Y.: Cornell University Press, 1992.

Salgado, Gamini. *Eyewitnesses of Shakespeare: First Hand Accounts of Performances, 1590–1890*. New York: Barnes and Noble, 1975.

Thomson, Peter. *Shakespeare's Professional Career*. Cambridge: Cambridge University Press, 1992.

Weimann, Robert. *Shakespeare and the Popular Tradition in the Theater: Studies in the Social Dimension of Dramatic Form and Function*. Edited by Robert Schwartz. Baltimore: Johns Hopkins University Press, 1978.

Yachnin, Paul. *Stage-Wrights: Shakespeare, Jonson, Middleton, and the Making of Theatrical Value*. Philadelphia: University of Pennsylvania Press, 1997.

Biography

Honigmann, F. A. J. *Shakespeare: The "Lost Years."* 2d ed. Manchester: Manchester University Press, 1998.

Schoenbaum, Samuel. *Shakespeare's Lives.* New ed. Oxford: Clarendon Press, 1991.

————. *William Shakespeare: A Compact Documentary Life*. Oxford: Oxford University Press, 1977.

General

Bergeron, David M., and Geraldo U. de Sousa. *Shakespeare: A Study and Research Guide*. 3d ed. Lawrence: University of Kansas Press, 1995.

Bradbey, Anne, ed. *Shakespearian Criticism, 1919–35*. London: Oxford University Press, 1936.

Colie, Rosalie L. *Shakespeare's Living Art*. Princeton, N.J.: Princeton University Press, 1974.

Grene, David. *The Actor in History: Studies in Shakespearean Stage Poetry*. University Park: Pennsylvania State University Press, 1988.

Goddard, Harold C. *The Meaning of Shakespeare*. 2 vols. Chicago: University of Chicago Press, 1951.

Kaufmann, Ralph J. *Elizabethan Drama: Modern Essays in Criticism*. New York: Oxford University Press, 1961.

McDonald, Russ. *The Bedford Companion to Shakespeare: An Introduction with Documents*. Boston: Bedford, 1996.

Raffel, Burton. *How to Read a Poem*. New York: Meridian, 1984.

Ricks, Christopher, ed. *English Drama to 1710*. Rev. ed. Harmondsworth: Sphere, 1987.

Siegel, Paul N., ed. *His Infinite Variety: Major Shakespearean Criticism Since Johnson*. Philadelphia: Lippincott, 1964.

Sweeting, Elizabeth J. *Early Tudor Criticism: Linguistic and Literary*. Oxford: Blackwell, 1940.

Van Doren, Mark. *Shakespeare*. New York: Holt, 1939.

FINDING LIST

Repeated unfamiliar words and meanings, alphabetically arranged, with act, scene, and footnote number of first occurrence, and in the spelling (form) of that first occurrence

aby	3.2.154	certain	1.1.106
against	1.1.139	chide	3.2.42
amend	2.1.160	chink	3.1.32
an	1.2.40	civil	2.1.193
anon	2.1.19	companion	1.1.21
aye	1.1.79	company	1.2.1
bank	2.1.245	compare	2.2.84
befall	1.1.74	confusion	1.1.172
before	1.1.51	corn	2.1.94
belike	1.1.145	counsel	1.1.232
beshrew	2.2.55	course	1.1.152
blood	1.1.72	dear	3.2.95
bold	1.1.70	decking	1.1.226
bosom	1.1.31	derision	3.2.111
brake	3.1.4	despised	2.2.64
by	2.1.34	devices	1.2.74